DEFINITION PROBLEM IN TERRORISM

DEFINITION PROBLEM IN TERRORISM

Caesar Roy

LL.M., PGDCFS

Assistant Professor of Law, Midnapore Law College

West Bengal

KALPAZ

ISBN: 978-93-5128-095-8

Price: ₹ 580

First Published, 2015

Published by

Kalpaz Publications
C-30, Satyawati Nagar,
Delhi – 110052
E-mail: kalpaz@hotmail.com
Ph.: 9212142040

Laser Typesetting: Lucky Graphic, Delhi
Printed at: G. Print Process, Delhi

Cataloging in Publication Data—DK
Courtesy: D.K. Agencies (P) Ltd. <docinfo@dkagencies.com>

Roy, Caesar, author.
Definition problem in terrorism / Caesar Roy, LL.M., PGDCFS.
pages cm
Includes bibliographical references and index.
ISBN 9789351280958

1. Terrorism—India. 2. Terrorism. I. Title.

DDC 303.6250954 23

Dedicated To

Lord Shirdi Sai Baba

for granting me the

strengh to write this book

Contents

Preface

Terrorism has turned into the most dominant danger to peace and security of each and every nation of the world. Though terrorism is a very common phenomenon of the world but there is no official or universal definition of terrorism agreed on all over the world. Despite decade of academic literature on the subject of terrorism no commonly accepted definition has been found. An appropriate definition of terrorism is the need of the hour to confront international terrorism. There are more than 100 definitions of the word 'terrorism'; these definitions are used at both international and regional levels as well as by various scholars. There are numbers of regional and international conventions which are related to terrorism. These conventions also tried to define a unanimous definition of terrorism. All those efforts make to define terrorism are doomed to failure and does not make possible to formulate a general acceptable and comprehensive definition of terrorism.

It shall be my endeavour to deal with almost all the definitions of terrorism and to search out necessity and obstacles to define terrorism and also the main ingredients of terrorism. The present book is in a analytical and critical commentary on the subject. Humble attempt has been made in the aforesaid area in the present book. The very title of this book "*Definition Problem in Terrorism*" gives just a little indication of its contents.

In writing this book, I enriched my knowledge by referring to various committee reports, articles from national and international journals, reference as well as text books, policy papers, internet materials etc. It will not be possible to acknowledge everyone. I record my immense gratitude to all the authors around the world.

To my parents, I owe what I am and everything I have. But for their enthusiastic encouragement, patience, sacrifice, strength and gentleness, I may have been lost in wilderness. I wish to put on record my thanks to my wife for her support during preparation of this book and to my son Drishan who gave up his claim to the time spent in writing this book.

I also take this opportunity of recording my appreciation and thanks to Kalpaz Publications for the interests and attention they have given to publish this book, without whose active co-operation the work would not have the shape of the book.

With legitimate expectations of a warm welcome from my readers, I present this book of mine for their valuable judgement. Any suggestion for the improvement of the book shall be highly appreciated and gratefully accepted.

The 27th July, 2014 **Caesar Roy**

1

INTRODUCTION

Defintion

What is the definition of terrorism? That is the question I shall tackle in this book, even if its interest may be highly controversial. That question may seem of the utmost importance, since terrorism has become one of the main concerns of present day societies and since it is easy to recognise but hard to define. The question of what terrorism is may, on the contrary, seem trifling and useless. As a matter of fact, terrorism continues to pervade the political system because there is no acceptable definition; and hence no punitive action against the perpetrator is possible either by the government or by the international organisations. The task of defining terrorism is not only very difficult, but also frustrating. It is a nightmare which has deeply distributed the conscience of mankind. It has come to symbolise the scourge of modern civilisation. Its internal and external linkages have made it a formidable challenge to the development, world peace and the very existence of humanity. Terrorism is an old problem with new challenges. It has drastically affected the world economy and people's life. It is a curse on human kind. Thousands of innocent persons, having no link with or knowledge of terrorist have lost their lives in terrorist attacks.

The terrorist attack on the World Trade Center in New York on 9/11 set in motion a new era all over the world– an era of a world uniting against a common enemy, but also an era of insecurity and fear. In formulating an effective counter-terrorist strategy, the construction of a universal definition of terrorism is needed. There is no doubt that we are all more united than ever in our effort to fight this universal war against terrorism. We all agree that the terrorist need to be hunted down and brought to justice wherever they are. It were incidents such as this that threatened to deprive the world's efforts from their true meaning and value and transform them to religious hatred. Despite the attempts that have been made internationally, to agree upon certain terms and plan a common strategy in the war against terrorism, the results are rather discouraging. Although, we all agree on the necessity of an internationally accepted definition of terrorism, we seem unable to succeed. One man's terrorist is another man's hero and one country's threat seems to be another country's salvation.

Terrorism is not a new phenomenon and even though it has been used since the beginning of recorded history, it can be relatively hard to define terrorism. There are innumerable definitions of terrorism and every definition though it appears correct in its own perspective, lacks some important aspects of terrorism. However, if these definitions are analysed in true sense, an acceptable definition could be evolved. There is no universally accepted definition of terrorism and even when people agree on a definition of terrorism, they sometimes disagree about whether or not the definition fits a particular incident. In order to understand terrorism, one must assess the different views of what exactly constitutes terrorism. Reaching a general conclusion on the definition of terrorism has generated much debate in the social sciences and in the international arena . No single definition seems to satisfy the wide interpretation of what specifically terrorism is. The problem of defining terrorism is compounded by the fact that terrorism has recently become a fad word used promiscuously and often applied to a variety of acts of violence which are not strictly terrorism by definition. Some governments are prone to label as terrorism all violent acts committed by their political opponents, while anti-government extremists frequently claim to be the victims of government terror. What is called terrorism thus seems to depend on one's point of view. In the absence of a definition, there is a free and open tendency for the persons using the term, whether states, organised groups or scholars, to define it as suits their purposes at the moment, leading to uncertainty as to how to fashion a legal structure to address terrorism. The difficulty in assigning a truly comprehensive definition to terrorism lies in the fact that, not only is it challenging to be specific when motives, targets and methods differ so broadly from case to case, but the complexity of untangling overlaps within each of these categories makes the task virtually impossible.

In this book, it is aimed to provide a review of existing academic definitions, conceptualise problems related to the attempts to arrive at a consensus on the definition in the field, and point to some potential avenues for establishing a deeper contextual understanding of the phenomenon. It is assumed that by means of presenting existing positions, internal and external tensions and major issues of contention, the following lines could contribute to an expansion of such a contextual understanding even if the polyphonic and dialectical character of the contemporary discourse is projected onto them.

Aristotle observed long ago that our definitional powers are essentially linked to our ability to distinguish good from evil. The gift of speech, Aristotle tells us, goes beyond the physical capacity to utter sounds and even the ability to recognise and name objects in the physical world. The essential attribute of human speech is captured by the ability to differentiate, categorise, and define a variety of incidents as belonging to a common genus, while excluding others. It is the capacity to distinguish and define which enables us to make ethical judgements.[1]

To bring this observation into the present context, the twenty-first-century philosopher's objective must be to define terrorism in order to identify its morally crucial features. Aside from pure moral inquiry, there are also other, more practical, objectives to be served by a clear definition of terrorism. Lawyers desperately require definitions in order to prosecute and sanction "terrorists." They must distinguish terrorism in precise legal terms from other forms of crime. Social scientists aim to describe this phenomenon in a way which will better our sociological and psychological understanding of it and enable us to face this modern challenge more successfully. Heads of state and politicians often adopt definitions that serve their national, political, or ideological agendas. Naturally, they usually define terrorism as a form of violence that is carried out exclusively by non-state groups.

So, to justify that the definition of terrorism seems not only necessary but also achievable. Without a definition of it, one could neither identify an act of violence as terrorist nor condemn (or justify) that act. Although there are many school of thoughts on terrorism, one can argue that the controversies among scholars and politicians about the very nature of terrorism are generally artificial. Actually, certain traits are constantly and unanimously attributed to terrorism, such that it seems possible to draw from them firm definitions of terrorism. Yet, even the most rigorous and precise of those definitions are nonetheless disappointing and insufficient. They are either too wide or too narrow and are often far from axiological neutrality. These so-called definitions of terrorism are in fact justifications or condemnations of certain forms of violence rather than adequate and exhaustive descriptions of the phenomenon. The definition of terrorism is vital as a means of fighting the terrorist threat, as well as serving as a guideline in the prosecutions of suspected terrorists. Understanding, and ultimately solving, the difficulties faced by those assessing the motivations of different terrorist groups, allows for a more thorough application of the definition of terrorism. Countering terrorism means predicting the methods used by groups and the likely targets; a truly thorough comprehension and definition of motivations would better serve this purpose.

Reference

1. Aristotle. (1976), *The Nicomahcaan Ethics,* London: Penguin Books, (pp. 75-76).

2

HISTORY OF TERRORISM

Although the subject of terrorism has always been and continues to be a hotly debated and widely interpreted issue but it is not a new form of violence. Terrorism is not a new thing. Indeed, in some respects, it predates by millennia. But the act of terrorism has remained static. Rather, as the difficulties involved in defining it reflect, terrorism has evolved considerably over the years, retaining some of the same characteristics that have historically typified it. Terrorism has been practised throughout history and throughout the world. Can the huge variety of forms of action be categorised under the single label of 'terrorist'? However, it is important that we should not ignore certain historical antecedents of terrorism and violence in order to appreciate the relationship between ancient and contemporary terrorist movements.

International Scenario

The origin of terrorism can be traced in ancient times. In ancient Greece the tyrants, though some of them were builders and patrons of arts, were looked down upon for their illegal and autocratic rule. Aristotle viewed tyranny as the worst form of perverted government, and tyrannicides in ancient Greece received the highest acclaim.[1] Recorded historical evidence supports terrorism's origins at about 2000 years with emergence of violent Jewish fanatical groups such as Sicarii.[2] However, the word 'terror' was first used to describe the Jacobin 'Reign of terror' that followed the French Revolution in 1789, and it was coined by Maximilien Rebespierre.[3] The period 1793 – 1794 is referred to as La Terreur (Reign of Terror). The terms terrorism and terrorist have their roots in the French Revolution. Since that time terrorism has been widely used to describe almost every form of violent behaviour. It was first used to describe political violence by a government against its citizen and political opponents.

Terrorism as a strategy to produce fear was first introduced by the Jewish Sicarii (dragger men) and Zealot movements of ancient Palestine. The Sicarii were Jewish religious zealots who instigated a popular uprising in Palestine between 66 and 70 AD. The Sicarii group used its favoured weapon, which was the Sica (a short dagger, which gave them their name, which literally means, 'dagger men'). The Sicarii and the Zealots, through acts of histrionic terror, successfully influenced a massive revolt against their colonial Roman rulers. The Zealots were generally targetting Romans and Greeks to kill and the killing usually took place in daylight and in front of witnesses in order to send a message to the Romans authorities and Jews, who collaborated with them. However, the revolt ended after the Romans had encircled the Sicarii at Masada. Fearing retaliation by the Romans in the form of torture and death, the Sicarii refused to surrender and ended the siege of Masada by engaging in a dramatic mass suicide. Nearly, a thousand Sicarii, including women and children, committed suicide rather than become Roman prisoners.[5]

A similar mixture of religious zeal and political extremism was the feature of a better known religious sect called the Assassins (a name that literally means *hashish* eater). The name Assassin is derived from the Arabic *hashashin,* or "*hashish*-eaters." The Assassins were under the influence of *hashish* when they envisioned paradise, when they attacked their targets, and when they went eagerly to their death. Indeed, because of the myth of their wide use of hashish, the members of the sect were called hashishin in Arabic; this name turned into "assassin". The Assassins practised the secret murder of their enemies from bases in Persia, Iraq and Syria, where hundreds of devoted followers directed the activities of dedicated terrorists. The Assassins realised that the success of their organisation depended on secrecy and a small number of dedicated followers to prevent detection from rival religious and political groups. So, they planned a long-term campaign of terror, often striking their victims at night while they slept. The Assassins were a division of the Shia Muslim sect known as the Nizari Ismailis, founded by Hasan al-Sabbah which was infamous for their use of murder to intimidate or eliminate their enemies. They used to stab their victim's in broad daylight.[6] Hassan-i-Sabbah, the founder of anti-Sunni sect, was poised to spread his brand of Ismaili Islam throughout the Middle East and defeat the Sunni rulers. Hasan and his followers first took control of a mountain fortress called Alamut, on the southern shore of the Caspian Sea. Hasan's goal was to return Islam to its fundamental roots, and he sent preachers throughout the region, to Baghdad, Damascus and Aleppo. He then sent out missionaries, who spread the order throughout Persia and Syria, and so was able to establish a power base among the outer tribes and mountain people. As Hasan's influence grew, he wanted to expand his empire and protect himself from his enemies as well. He did not have the military power to confront his enemies directly, so he simply had them eliminated by killers, who were able to infiltrate the enemy defences by disguise and deception. Sometimes they would even join the enemy leader's inner circle of advisors or personal bodyguards, and wait patiently – sometimes for several years – for the signal to strike. When the moment came to dispatch the intended victim, they would stab him to death with a knife, and then instead of trying to escape, they would calmly await their fate. Hasan and his successors were so successful at eliminating their enemies, that they were greatly feared throughout the Middle East and in parts of Asia, Africa and Europe as well. He convinced his fanatically devoted followers that actively fighting for their cause would assure them a place in paradise. Recognising that their membership was too small to fight their enemies openly the Assassins operated clandestinely until the assigned member or members attacked a prominent leader – typically in front of large crowds. They assaulted their targets with daggers and made no attempt to escape but seemed content, even eager, to be caught and killed after they had accomplished their dangerous missions. Thus, in today's parlance, the Assassins practised a form of "suicide terrorism." This group continued its operations till the middle of the 13th century when they were destroyed by the Mongols.

The word terrorism comes from the 'Reign of Terror', instigated by Maxmilien Robespierre in 1793, following the French revolution. The French Revolution provided the first uses of the words "Terrorist" and "Terrorism" Use of the word "terrorism" began in 1795 in reference to the 'Reign of Terror' initiated by the Revolutionary government.[7] The word was born with the 'Reign of Terror' the use of the guillotine by the French revolutionaries to consolidate their regime by killing their enemies and intimidating the potential opposition. In June 1793, the French Revolution enters its most violent and turbulent phase when the Jacobins seized control of the National Convention from the more moderate Girondins had instituted a series of radical measures, including the establishment of a new calendar and the eradication of Christianity. This was a commonly held belief in 1793-1794, when the guillotine was a means of purging France of those who were deemed a threat to national security. They also unleashed the bloody 'Reign of Terror' a 10-month period in which suspected enemies of the revolution were guillotined by the thousands.[8] Many of the killings were carried out under orders from Robespierre, who dominated the draconian Committee of Public Safety until his own execution on July 28, 1794.

In the nineteenth century, the terms were applied to violence of the agrarian agitation against landlords and their agents in Ireland. Later in that century, the terms were linked to the strategy of political assassinations employed by the anti-Tsarist Russian movement '*Narodnaya Volya*' (People's Will) against the Tsarist regime.[9] *Narodnaya Volya* was organised in 1879 by members of the revolutionary Populist Party, *Zemlyai-volya* ("Land and Freedom"), who were disillusioned by the failure of their efforts to promote social revolution by agitating among peasants. The new group, emphasising the need for an organised political struggle against the state structure, used terror to force political reform as well as to undermine the state. From 1866 to 1881 several terrorist attempts were made culminating in the assassination of Alexander II on March, 1881. The assassins were arrested and hanged. The murder of the emperor stimulated anti-terrorist sentiment in Russia, and *Narodnaya Volya*, its ranks already decimated by mass arrests, collapsed in the following year.[10] Another political ideology closely linked to terrorism is the anarchist tradition of assassination. Anarchism has frequently been associated with terrorism. Anarchists, who believe in abolishing all government, were very active throughout Europe during the late nineteenth and early twentieth centuries. The most notorious anarchist group was the Russian anarchists group, *Narodnaya Volya,* as stated above. They propagated what has remained the common terrorist delusion that violent acts would spark off revolution. In the following century the bomb throwing anarchist, who held the notion of 'Propaganda by deed', came to be seen as the terrorist. 'Propaganda by deed' is the idea that social regeneration can be achieved only through acts that inspire dread and horror in those presently controlling the institutions of social order. This established a link between anarchism and terrorism, which gave the interpretation of ideology to terrorism.[11]

Propaganda became an essential feature of anarchism, because making the public aware of the movement was necessary. As Paul Brousse, a leading French anti-parliamentarian, who coined the phrase 'propaganda by deed', argued that the propaganda through news media or public meetings was of limited value because the hard working masses had little time or inclination to attend to intellectual modes of communications. What was necessary was a practical demonstration (i.e., a 'deed') which could not be ignored.

Kropotkin, in 1870, formulated anarchist action as constant agitation by any possible means – including the gun and the bomb. A couple of anarchists even believed that no one is innocent, and the victims of anarchist attacks, in most of the cases, really were ordinary citizens guilty of no capitalist crimes.[12]

According to anarchist theory; the masses are asleep and need to be awakened so that they can be unified to revolt. In other words, terrorism would stir the spirit of revolt within the masses. The use of terrorism will communicate to the masses that they can revolt, as well as communicating to the ruling class that they are not beyond the reach of the people, who resist their oppression. As Laqueur recounts of *Narodnaya Volya* theory, "If ten or fifteen of the establishment were killed at one time and the same time, the government would panic and would lose its freedom of action. At the same time, the masses would wake up."[13] As a movement, anarchism survived until World War-I in Russia and until the beginning of World War-II in Spain.

Terrorism continued for many decades to be associated primarily with the assassination of political leaders and heads of state. Between the late 1940s and the 1960s, terrorism changed from selectively targetting government officials to targetting civilians. As the Cold War escalated in the 1960s, with the world polarised between East and West, a new dynamic developed in transnational terrorism, state-sponsored terrorism: government exported terrorism to other parts of the world for their own political interests. Iran supported Hezbollah; Libya supported Abu Nidal; and Iraq, Cuba, Sudan and Algeria provided training camps, as well as economic and political support to terrorist groups around the world. Terrorism moved to the Middle East and the Arab–Israeli conflict, with the United States supporting Israel, and the Soviet Union supporting various Arab countries. It was during this time that terrorists begun choosing airplanes as targets. The 1970s were known as the decade of air terrorism, with more than 20 hijacking, bombing and hostage taking incidents directed against European and American airlines. The 1970s also experienced bombings, kidnappings and other types of terrorist activity throughout Europe.

It is said that the age of modern terrorism have begun in the year 1968 when the Popular Front for the Liberation of Palestine (PFLP) hijacked an El Al airliner *en route* from Tel Aviv to Rome. While hijackings of airliners had occurred before, this was the first time that the nationality of the carrier (Israeli) and its symbolic value was a specific operational aim. Also a first was the deliberate use of the passengers as hostages for demands made publicly against the Israeli government. The combination of these unique events, added to the international scope of the operation, gained significant media attention. The founder of PFLP, Dr George Habash observed that the level of coverage was tremendously greater than battles with Israeli soldiers in their previous area of operations.

International terrorism is considered to have gotten its start at the 1972 Summer Olympics in Munich, West Germany. 'Black September', a Palestinian group, kidnapped and killed Israeli athletes preparing to compete. 'Black September's' political goal was negotiating the release of Palestinian prisoners. They used spectacular tactics to bring international attention to their national cause.

The 1980s were known as a decade of hostage taking, with terrorism finding a target in American interests around the world. These incidents included the 1979 hostage crisis, bombing of United

States embassies, kidnapping of American citizens and bombing of airplanes.

Between 1993 and September 11, 2001, seven Middle Eastern-inspired terrorist attacks were committed against the United States, with destruction as their goal. The first World Trade Center attack in 1993, claimed six lives and caused major building damage. In 1995, a car bomb left five dead at the United States military headquarters in Saudi Arabia; and in 1996, also in Saudi Arabia, 19 died in at the Khobar Towers. In 1997, 58 tourists were killed when terrorists opened fire in the Temple of Hatshepsut in Egypt. In Kenya and Tanzania, 224 died in the simultaneous 1998 bombings of two United States embassies. In Yemen, 17 sailors were killed by the attack on the USS Cole in 2000. Finally, in 2001, the World Trade Center and Pentagon attacks killed an estimated 3000 people.

Indian Scenario

The first ruler of the ancient Maurya empire in India, Chandragupta Maurya (340 BC – 298 BC) was the first to pay close attention to national security, and preferred wielding the '*danda*', that is using fear in a near-totalitarian way. 14 Muslim period marked the beginning of new era in the history of India. Arabs were the first Muslims who came to India. The Muslim dominated Kabul, the Punjab, and Sind, before intruding into India. The wealth in India lured the Muslim rulers. Further the inter-rivalry between the kingdoms in India paved the way for their entry into India. The very first Muslim attack on India in Sindh in the year 715 A.D. was by Arabs, led by Mohammad Bin Qasim. They displaced Raja Dahir, who ruled Sindh from his capital Deval (near modern Karachi). The unprovoked attacks over the Hindus by the Ghaznis and Ghoris can be tremed as terrorist attack. They caused terror among the Hindus as they indulged in acts of mere vandalism and brutality.[15]

In the Medieval Period, one of the remarkable person who spurred by to great ambition to rob power by force was Genghis Khan (1162–1227) with his fast moving horsemen, went across Asia. He was a Mongolian tribal. He was such a terror that he was irresistible and involved in bloodshed and brutal killing of human beings.[16] Genghis Khan dealt with his enemies with all ferocity and was able to create a fearful situation among the enemies. Genghis Khan formed a systematic warring system to face the enemies in an aggressive and violent manner.[17]

The Indian emperors ruled India till the beginning of sixteenth century. The fall of India took place in 1526 AD when Babur (1483 – 1530) invaded India by defeating Ibrahim Lodi at Panipat and established Mughal Empire in India in 1526 AD.[18] Babur organized his troops for the battle in the same manner what the Mongolian conqueror Genghis Khan did. It was not only that Babur, but almost all the Mughal kings did the same thing, made grave bloodshed battles, maintained terrorism in their kingdoms. During the period, Mughals it was not only in battles terrorism prevailed, but also in the day to day life situations. The Mughals kings converted the Hindus in India by terrorising them at the point of sword. Innocent people were put into serious consequences to adapt Muslim religious rites.[19] Among the successors of Mughal dynasty, Akbar (1526 – 1605) followed the policy of conquest for the expansion of his empire. However, Aurangzeb extended empire; he could not conquer the whole Indian Peninsula. There were the Hindu Kingdoms in Rajasthan, Gujarat and Maharastra regions. The Mughal's victory over other regions was due to the faction among the Muslims themselves. The splendour and luxury of the Mughal emperors produced rebellions among the people of the neighbouring regions, the Rajput and the Marathas.[20] Maharana Pratap, a Hindu Rajput ruler of Mewar, was one of the great rebels of the Mughals. Mewar, where the Rajput spirit had manifested itself in its very quintessence, which had been provided with excellent means of defence in its steep mountains and strong castles and which had contested with Babur the supremacy of Northern India, did not bow his head. Rana Pratap led the Rajputs against the army of Akbar to preserve the independence of Mewar. In the Battle of Haldighati (1576) fought between Maharana Pratap and the Mughals; the Rajputs were not able to overcome the combined strength of the Mughals. Although Maharana Pratap was not able to thwart the Muslims successfully, the saga of Rajput resistance to Muslim rule continued till the 17th century, when the baton of the struggle for Indian Independence from Mughals was taken up by the upcoming power of the Marathas, who brought about an end to Muslim domination of India.

The British set up their first Indian trading post in 1619, and the British East India Company grew increasingly influential over the following century. British rule in India said to have started in 1757 when at the battle of Plassey forces of the English East India Company defeated the Nawab of Bengal Siraj-ud-Daulla. The Indians at every stage tried to protest against the British rule and on the other side the struggle was suppressed with great violence and the British created an atmosphere of terror in the country. Hundreds were executed without trial. There was hardly any region in northern India where corpses, hanging from gibbets, did not remind the people of the vengeance of the British Government.

Anti-terrorism legislations have been part of the legal scene in India since the time of British. These legislations are, moreover, entirely similar to special laws that have been enacted from time to time to deal with special situations. The first preventive detention law was introduced by the British in 1793, and was aimed solely for the purpose of detaining anybody, who was regarded as a threat to the British settlement in India. East India Company Act, 1793 authorised the Governor of Fort William to detain any citizen on suspicion that he was carrying on any illicit correspondence dangerous to the peace and security of the British Settlement in India under the Bengal State Prisoners Regulation of 1818 also known as Notorious Bengal Regulation-III and similar enactments in Madras and Bombay which laid no fetters upon the powers of the government to detain a person on suspicion.[21] An extra-constitutional ordinance, opposed to all the fundamental liberties which the colonial state would later pretend to be bound by Regulation-III provided for the indefinite confinement of individuals against whom there was insufficient ground to institute any judicial proceeding. Regulation-III was the most effective tool in the hands of the British to quell any political violence.

Indian soldiers serving the British Indian Army were discontented and there was resentment among them. Hundred years of popular discontent took the form of armed resistance, led by the deposed chieftains of their descendants and relations, zamindars and poligars and ex-soldiers, officials and other retainers of Indian states. Large section of the peasantry and artisans joined these revolts, because of their grievances and hardships, often forming the backbone of these revolts. These civil rebellions began with the very establishment of British rule in Bengal and Bihar. Intensification of the land revenue demand, exploitation of the artisans by the East India Company and its servants and the uprooting of old zamindars created explosive situation. The most relevant widespread of peasant movement was the Indigo Revolt of 1859-60. The government had to mobilise a large network of soldier and armed policemen to suppress the peasant movement. Many peasants were killed in brutal firings and bayonet charges. It came about in the twentieth century when the discontent of the peasant masses was merged with the general anti-imperialist discontent and their potential activity found expression in under the national movement and the modern Kisan movements.

Following the 1857, Indian uprising and the consolidation of British control, the Indian Council Act of 1861, which was the statute establishing the overall governance framework for British India, authorised the Governor General to legislate outside the ordinary law-making process in emergency situations by unilaterally issuing ordinances to ensure "the peace and good government" of India. Such ordinances frequently were used to authorise administrative detention and to establish special tribunals to adjudicate cases relating to law and order, especially during wartime.[22] Two subsequent framework statutes, the Government of India Acts of 1919 and 1935, also granted the Governor General emergency ordinance-making authority based on similar criteria.

In addition to this general emergency, ordinance-making authority, the British enacted special emergency legislation during the two World Wars. During World War-I, the British enacted the Defence of India Act of 1915, which adapted the wartime "emergency code" from Britain for use in India and authorised the Governor General in Council to issue rules to secure the public safety and defence of British India. The Act authorised civil and military authorities to detain individuals or impose other restraints on personal liberty if they had "reasonable grounds" to suspect a person's conduct was "prejudicial to public safety." The Defence of India Act, 1915 was enacted during World War-I and after the War; there were administrators, who felt that the sweeping powers provided by that law should be applicable in peacetime as well. A second Defence of India Act was enacted in

1939, at the outset of World War-II, authorising the government to preventively detain anyone whose conduct was likely "prejudicial to the defence of British India, the public safety, the maintenance of public order. Special tribunals were established to adjudicate violations of the Act's wartime rules, which remained in effect until they lapsed in October 1946. But the British never limited their use of such extraordinary powers in India to formally declared periods of emergency. As early as 1818, a regulation in Bengal empowered the government to detain anybody on mere suspicion.[23] The 1818 regulation ultimately was extended throughout India. Subject to minor amendments, it remained in effect even for several years after independence, before being superseded by new legislation conferring similar authority.

Before the end of World War-I, the British began to explore ways to preserve during peacetime the wartime emergency powers authorised by the Defence of India Act, 1915. Based on the recommendations of Justice Rowlatt, Chairman of the Committee appointed to curb rebellious movements in India the government in 1919, enacted the Anarchical and Revolutionary Crimes Act, known as the "Rowlatt Act". It did not define anarchical and revolutionary crimes and was thus open to grave misuse. The Act conferred broad power upon the government to combat "anarchical and revolutionary movements," a term the law did not define. Despite the lapse of the Defence of India Act and the end of the war, the Act preserved detention orders and other restraints on freedom of movement entered under that law's wartime authority. The Act also conferred new authority to order preventive detention or other restrictions on freedom of movement for up to two years of any individuals, who the government had reasonable grounds to believe were involved in an anarchical or revolutionary movement or, in parts of the country designated by the government as "affected areas," were suspected of connection to certain specified criminal offenses. While individuals subject to preventive detention were afforded an opportunity to appear before an investigating authority and learn the basis for their detention, such proceedings were not governed by the procedural and evidentiary protections governing regular criminal proceedings, such as the right to representation by counsel.[24]

In addition to authorising preventive detention and other restraints on free movement, the Rowlatt Act defined particular substantive criminal offenses and set forth special procedures to adjudicate those offenses, if the government determined that (1) anarchical and revolutionary movements were being promoted in all or part of India, and (2) the specified offenses were related to those movements and sufficiently prevalent to justify special, expedited procedures. Special courts were established to try such offenses, and ordinary procedural protections did not apply – the Act authorised in camera trial proceedings and eliminated the right to appeal. However, the law did ensure some judicial oversight over the exercise of prosecutorial discretion, requiring the government to provide its allegations to the chief justice of the High Court, who had discretion to seek additional facts before deciding whether to constitute a special court to adjudicate the alleged violation.[25]

With its extension of draconian wartime powers into an ordinary, non-emergency period, the Rowlatt Act became a focal point of the non-cooperation campaign, led by Mahatma Gandhi in the early 1920s.[26] In the face of this intense popular opposition, the government tempered its policies and permitted the *Rowlatt Act* to lapse in 1922. The British continued to use short-term Ordinances, however, to impose similar provisions on their subjects in India. However, the British did not refrain from exercising emergency-like powers during peacetime. To the contrary, the government continued to exercise preventive detention authority throughout the 1920s under the pre-existing 1818 regulation. When faced once again with large scale, nationwide civil disobedience during the 1930s, the government resumed and intensified its use of repressive powers and issuing ordinances. The most far-reaching of these ordinances, the *Emergency Powers Ordinance*, was issued in January 1932, when the government determined to crack down on the nationalist movement more aggressively.

The establishment of elected, semi-autonomous provincial governments under the *Government of India Act of 1935*, maintained the basic pattern established by the British. The Act explicitly granted the provincial legislatures authority to enact preventive detention laws of their own, and while the newly-elected, Congress-led governments initially made efforts to repeal the emergency powers enacted before

1935, by 1937 they increasingly began to rely upon the same kinds of measures used by the British to maintain order and exercise social control.[27] Between 1946 and 1950, under circumstances similar to those surrounding enactment of the Rowlatt Act, nearly all of the provincial governments responded to the lapse of the rules promulgated under the *Defence of India Act of 1939* by enacting "public safety acts" authorising preventive detention in the absence of a formally declared emergency. The 1935 legislation also strengthened the colonial executive's emergency powers by permitting it to supersede provincial authority if it determined that the "constitutional machinery" within a province had failed.[28] The Rules made under the *Defence of India Act, 1939* were to provide the power of detention and to keep it beyond the judicial review. Rule 26 of the Rules framed under the Defence of India Act of 1939, authorised the government to detain a person whenever it was satisfied with respect to that particular person that such detention was necessary to prevent him from acting in any manner prejudicial to the defence and safety to the country and the like. This Act was modelled on similar legislation in England as a measure during the World War-II.[29] The Preventive Detention Act was a temporary Act. Originally, it was passed only for one year. Several times since then the term of the Act was extended until it expired at the end of 1969.

The origin of the present day terrorism can be traced to the Sinai War of June 1967, when in a few days Israel decimated the armed forces of some of the Middle East countries and occupied large tract of their land. The Arab world has since then been simmering with anger and rage leading to the beginning of "contemporary wave of terrorism" in the Middle East in 1968. The first manifestation of moving away from the conventional war and confrontation between the Israeli and the Arab was the seizure of an American Airline by a Palestinian sympathiser.[30]

A study of the early history of terrorism in India shows that there are quite a few communities and groups in India, who have a long history of taking to terrorism to vindicate their honour. A few of these are Bengalees, Marathas and Sikhs. It were Sikhs, settled in British Columbia and on the west coast of the United States, who hatched the conspiracy to secure the freedom of India and to throw out the British by a campaign of terror. The educated Hindus were their leaders. The master plan of the GHADAR ('rebellion' in Punjabi) party was entrusted with many acts relating to conspiracy. The conspiracy progressed considerably but as it was hatched on US soil it collapsed after April, 1917 when USA joined Britain in the war against Germany. The GHADAR leaders were arrested, tried and sentenced to long jail terms.[31]

The two eminent leaders of the Indian national movement, who made terrorism respectable and attractive, were Bal Gangadhar Tilak and Aurobindo Ghose. To rouse the Maratha spirit, he revived the Ganapati festival and here worship of Shivaji. The sacred book of the Hindus, Bhagwat Gita, became the religious justification for killing enemies in a sacred cause. One of the prominent pupils of Tilak was Aurobindo Ghose, who went to Bengal to revive the terrorist movement there. One of the inciters of the revolutionaries in India was a journal, called *Bande Mataram,* in Paris. It openly exhorted revolutionaries to kill British and Indian officials.[32]

One of the first Acts of independent India was the *Madras Suppression of Disturbances Act,* 1948, which authorised the use of military violence against the peasants in Telengana. The peasant struggle in Telengana which began in 1946 was against forced labour, illegal extractions, evictions by feudal landlords and oppression by village Patels, among other things and later developed into an agrarian liberation struggle to get rid of feudal landlordism and the Nizam's dynastic rule in the state. The struggle continued even after the Nizam's rule ended with the entry of Indian troops in September 1948, and the merger of the Hyderabad State into the Indian Union.

The peasantry in about 3,000 villages, consisting roughly a population of three million in an area of about 16,000 square miles, mostly in the three districts of Nalgonda, Warangal and Khammam, succeeded in setting up gram-raj. The landlords were driven away from the villages, their lands seized, and one million acres of land were redistributed among the peasantry. As many as 4,000 Communists and peasant activists were killed and more than 10,000 Communist and sympathisers were put behind the bars.

In subsequent years, a large number of similar types of laws were passed, all of which provided legal cover for terrorising the populace.

From 1947 to 1975, independent India followed the same basic pattern established by the British in its use of emergency and security laws. While India's post-independence Constitution includes an extensive array of fundamental rights protections, its emergency and security provisions incorporate a number of the same basic principles found in the *Government of India Act* of 1935: extraordinary powers that may be exercised during declared periods of emergency, but supplemented by several layers of preventive detention and other security laws that readily afford the government multiple options to exercise similar powers even outside of formally declared periods of emergency. Between 1950 and 1975, the Central Government exercised its authority to declare a formal state of emergency twice – in 1962, when Chinese and Indian armed forces clashed along India's northern border, and in 1971, when war broke out between India and Pakistan.[33] Each of the two wartime proclamations of emergency was followed by parliamentary action conferring sweeping powers upon the executive. Rules promulgated under the *Defence of India Act of 1962*, for example, authorised the Central and State Governments to engage in preventive detention extending well beyond the length of time permitted under ordinary preventive detention laws.[34] While the rules established a system of administrative supervision and review, they set no maximum period of detention, and detainees were not entitled to learn the grounds for detention or to challenge the detention in any forum. The rules also authorised restrictions on freedom of movement and freedom of assembly; conferred broad search, seizure, and warrantless arrest powers upon magistrates and the police; increased penalties for a number of criminal offenses; and, to adjudicate violations, authorised the creation of special tribunals in which many ordinary criminal procedural protections were not available.[35] The government also suspended judicial enforcement of rights that may have been violated under the emergency proclamation.[36] While the formal ground for invoking the Constitution's emergency authority in each instance was war and external aggression, in each case the government maintained the state of emergency long after armed conflict had ceased, echoing efforts by the British to extend into peacetime the sweeping emergency powers authorised on account of war. Although, the conflict with China was over within days, the 1962 emergency proclamation remained in effect until 1968.[37]

Similarly, the 1971 war with Pakistan ended within weeks, and relations between India and Pakistan were soon normalised, yet the 1971 emergency proclamation remained in effect, along with a concurrent state of emergency declared by Indira Gandhi in 1975, in response to threats allegedly posed by "internal disturbance," through 1977.

Within weeks after the Constitution went into force, Parliament enacted the Preventive Detention Act of 1950, which authorised detention for up to twelve months by both the Central and State Governments, if necessary to prevent an individual from acting in a manner prejudicial to the defence or security of India, India's relations with foreign powers, state security or maintenance of public order, or maintenance of essential supplies and services. The act also implemented the limited procedural protections required by the Constitution. The PDA was originally set to expire after one year. However, as with the use of formal emergency authority, it was routinely reenacted each year for almost twenty years. While it finally lapsed in 1969, preventive detention authority returned less than two years later under the *Maintenance of Internal Security Act,* 1971 which largely restored the provisions of the PDA. The National Integration Council appointed a Committee on National Integration and Regionalisation to look into, the aspect of putting reasonable restrictions in the interests of the sovereignty and integrity of India. Pursuant to the acceptance of recommendations of the Committee, the Constitution (Sixteenth Amendment) Act, 1963 was enacted to impose, by law, reasonable restrictions in the interests of the sovereignty and integrity of India. In order to implement the provisions of 1963 Act, the Unlawful *Activities (Prevention) Bill* was introduced in the Parliament. The *Unlawful Activities (Prevention) Bill* having been passed by both the Houses of Parliament received the assent of the President on 30th December, 1967 and became the *Unlawful Activities (Prevention) Act, 1967.*

During the emergency period, i.e., from June 1975 to March 1977, India witnessed one of the darkest moments in the post-independence period. The excesses of the Emergency have cast a long shadow on the use of extraordinary laws against terrorism and other security threats in the years since then. MISA and other preventive detention laws were amended during the Emergency to permit much longer periods of detention, to make it easier for the government to exercise detention authority without Advisory Board scrutiny, and to eliminate other procedural protections that otherwise applied.[38] In the wake of the Emergency, the Janata-led government amended the Constitution to rein in the government's authority to exercise extraordinary powers, repealing some of the constitutional changes made during the Emergency and adding additional safeguards. During the summer of 1978, well over a year after taking office, this government finally repealed MISA. Upon the return to power of the Congress Party following elections in early 1980, the Congress government issued a sweeping preventive detention ordinance to replace MISA, which ultimately was replaced by an act of Parliament, the National Security Act of 1980.

During the Emergency, leaders of the Akali Dal, a leading Sikh political party, were among Indira Gandhi's sharpest critics, and after the 1977 elections, the party joined the Janata-led government that assumed power. The Congress Party when returned to power in 1980, extensive negotiations were made for several years between the Central government and the Akali Dal but failed to resolve their differences. In the meantime, both civil disobedience and violence in Punjab escalated sharply, including attacks by militant Sikhs against Hindu and moderate Sikh politicians and civilians and communal violence between Hindus and Sikhs. The Sikh demanded Khalistan, a separate country for India's Sikhs carved out of the (Indian) Punjab province. Hindu revivalist claimed Sikhism to be another branch of Hinduism as the Sikhs insisted on having separate identity. Report of the Government census of 1911-1921, showed that out of two dozen Sikh sects in Punjab in the beginning of the century, moved towards more unified and monolithic '*Keshdhari*' Sikh identity. Sant Bhindranwala and his disciples had begin to fortify the *Akal Takht* and the Golden Shrine (Temple) at Amritsar – two of the most shrines of the Sikhs – in anticipation of an attack by the Indian army.[39]

In September 1981, a group of Sikh separatists had taken refuge in the *Golden Shrine*, one of the most revered shrines of Sikhism. In June 1984, the Central Government imposed a curfew and deployed the military throughout Punjab as part of "Operation Bluestar," an operation involving a massive offensive by the Army and central paramilitary forces against militants in the Golden Shrine complex. The overwhelming use of force caused tremendous death and destruction. Unofficial estimates place the numbers of civilians killed in the thousands, including priests, pilgrims, and temple employees and their family members. The offensive also caused extensive damage to the temple complex itself. Many thousands more were detained throughout the state in the aftermath of the offensive. In October 1984, Indira Gandhi was assassinated by two Sikh bodyguards, and in the aftermath of her death, thousands of Sikhs were killed and tens of thousands displaced in targetted violence.

The government extensively used the NSA throughout the early 1980s, and in October 1983, the government dismissed the Punjab state government and imposed President's Rule. The government also amended the NSA in early 1984 to permit it to be used more aggressively in Punjab, extending the maximum period of detention from one year to two years, extending the deadline for referral to an Advisory Board from three months to four-and-a-half months.

In early 1984, Parliament enacted the *Terrorist Affected Areas (Special Courts) Act, 1984* which established special courts to adjudicate certain "scheduled offences" related to terrorism in areas designated by the Central government, for specified time periods, as "terrorist affected." Most of the provisions of the said Act were incorporated into the more sweeping *Terrorist and Disruptive Activities (Prevention) Act of 1985,* which was enacted in the wake of Indira Gandhi's assassination.

In addition to Central laws, there are also laws which are applicable to specific territories. Many States have passed *Control of Organised Crime Acts*, such as *Maharashtra Control of Organised Crime Act, 1999* and there is also the controversial *Armed Forces Special Powers Acts* which are in force in certain areas with the view to combat terrorism. The *Armed Forces (Assam and Manipur) Special Powers Act, 1958* is one of the earliest repressive laws (after Preventive Detention) to be introduced in post-independence India. The Act guarantees impunity to the armed forces that no prosecution, etc., shall be instituted except with the previous sanction of the Central government against any person. It allows armed forces to fire upon, even causing death of any person, who is acting in contravention of any law if the person is of the opinion that it is necessary for public order. It also allows arrest without warrant of any person against whom a reasonable suspicion arises.[40]

Like other countries, the terrorist attacks on September 11, 2001, affected the political dynamics in India also. India formulated a Bill in the form of ordinance on 24th October, 2001, the *Prevention of Terrorism Ordinance, 2001*, temporarily deferring full parliamentary consideration of the proposal. In the midst of the debate over the proposed bill, the government's proposal gained further momentum from two significant terrorist attacks – an attack on the legislative assembly complex in the state of Jammu and Kashmir in October 2001, and an assault on the Indian Parliament building in Delhi in December 2001. The debate over the proposed legislation was highly charged. Despite vigorous opposition, Parliament ultimately affirmed the government's ordinance, enacting the *Prevention of Terrorism Act, 2002 (POTA)* into law in March 2002, during an extraordinary joint session of both houses of Parliament. In 2004 itself, certain amendments were introduced to the *Unlawful Activities (Prevention) Act, 1967*, thereby making it the nation's anti-terror legislation. In the aftermath of the spurt in the terrorist activities recent years including the Parliamentary attack and the Mumbai attacks, the government introduced the *Unlawful Activities (Prevention)* Amendment Bill in Lok Sabha on 16th December, 2008, aiming to strengthen the arrangements for speedy investigation, prosecution and trial of cases related to terrorism. The Bill was passed by Lok Sabha and became the law of the land on 17th December, 2008. This Act was further amended in the year 2012 by the Unlawful Activities (Prevention) Amendment Act, 2012[41] which includes economic offences within the ambit of terror acts.

References

1. Sen, S. (1994). *Terrorism and Drugs* (p. 1). Kolkata: S.C. Sarkar.
2. Mark Burgess, "*A Brief History of Terrorism*," Center for Defence Information (July 2, 2003). Retrieved January 10, 2012 from www.cdi.org/friendlyversion/printversion.cfm?documentID=1502.

3. *Ibid.*
4. Horsley, R. (1979). The Sicarii: Ancient Jewish Terrorists, *The Journal of Religion,* 59(4), Chicago: Chicago University Press, pp. 435-458.
5. *Brandon*, S.G.F. (1967). *Jesus and the Zealots*: *A Study of the Political Factor in Primitive Christianity* (p. 56). Manchester: Manchester University *Press.*
6. Jeffrey, S (2001). *The Terrorist Trap* (pp. 26-27). Bloomington: Indiana University Press, 2001.
7. Golder, B, and Williams, G. (2004). What Is terrorism? Problems of legal definition. *UNSW Law Journal*, Sydney: The University of New South Wales, p. 270.
8. Griset, P., and Mahan, S. (2003). *Terrorism in Perspective*. (p. 4). London: Sage Publication.
9. Bhattacharya, S. (2007). *Terrorism and Moral Questions* (p. 3). Kolkata: Sarat Book Distributors.
10. Saxena, N.S. (1985). *Terrorism History and Facets in the World and in India* (p. 44). New Delhi: Abhinav Publication.
11. Bhattacharya, S. (2007). *Terrorism and Moral Questions* (p. 3). Kolkata: Sarat Book Distributors.
12. *Ibid.*
13. Laqueur, W. (1977). *Terrorism*. (p. 34). Boston: Little, Brown, and Company.
14. Kennedy, T., Blackwell, F., Chan, Roger Y. M., & Nitz, T., (1996). Incorporating Asia in the General Education Curriculum. *Education about Asia, 1(2).* Retrieved January 18, 2012 from https://www.asian-studies.org/eaa/kennedy.htm.
15. Srivastava, A.L. (1976). *The Sultanate of Delhi* (pp. 394-398). Agra: Shiva Lal Agarwala & Co.
16. Rajamanickam, M. (2009). *Psychological Perspective of International Terrorism* (p. 59). New Delhi: Concept Publishing Company.
17. *Ibid.* p. 60.
18. *Ibid.* p. 62.

19. *Ibid.* pp. 62-63.

20. *Ibid.* pp. 65-66.

21. Singh, Dr. K. (2010). *Human Rights and Anti-Terrorism Laws in India* (p. 29). New Delhi: Central Law Publications.

22. Iyer, V. (2000). *States of Emergency: The Indian Experience* (pp. 67-68). New Delhi: Butterworth.

23. *The Hindu*, dated 7th September, 2004.

24. Iyer, V. (2000). *States of Emergency: The Indian Experience* (p. 68). New Delhi: Butterworth.

25. Iyer, V. (2000). *States of Emergency: The Indian Experience* (p. 68). New Delhi: Butterworth.

26. Sarkar, S. (2000). *Modern India: 1885-1947* (pp. 187-195). Mumbai: Macmillan Publishers India.

27. *Ibid., page* 352.

28. *Ibid., page* 376.

29. Singh, Dr. K. (2010). *Human Rights and Anti-Terrorism Laws in India* (p. 29). New Delhi: Central Law Publications.

30. *Ibid., page* 29.

31. Saxena, N. S. (1985). *Terrorism History and Facets in the World and in India* (pp. 25-26). New Delhi: Abhinav Publication.

32. *Ibid., page* 26.

33. Iyer, V. (2000). *States of Emergency: The Indian Experience* (p. 141). New Delhi: Butterworth.

34. *Ibid., page* 109.

35. *Ibid., pages* 109-114.

36. *Ibid., page* 105.

37. *Ibid., page* 125.

38. *Ibid.,* pp. 167-170.

39. Singh, Dr. K. (2010). *Human Rights and Anti-Terrorism Laws in India* (p. 37). New Delhi: Central Law Publications.

40. Haragopal, G., and Jagannatham, B. (2009). Terrorism and

Human Rights: Indian Experiment with Repressive Laws, *Economic and Political Weekly, 44*. Mumbai. p. 76.

41. Received the assent of the President on 03.01.2013 and published in the Gazette of India, Extra, Part II, Section 1, dated 04.01.2013. Came into force on 01.02.2013, vide S.O. 294(E), dated 31.01.2013.

3

THEORIES AND DIFFERENT KINDS OF TERRORISM

Theories of Terrorism

There are so many theories of terrorism, which are mentioned below to provide a context to best understand the theoretical basis of terrorism. The history of theoretical effort at understanding terrorism comes from the sub-field of collective violence in the field of political science, and indeed, prior to the emergence of criminal justice as a separate discipline in the early 1970s, it can be safely said that political science pretty much had a monopoly over theories of terrorism, followed perhaps by the disciplines of religion and economics. Sociological, psychological, and criminological theories have also certainly had a role to play with some relevance.[1] This may help to arrive at an understanding of the problem of tackling terrorism.

(i) Theory of Anarchism

Terrorism is most definitely not a form of governance, but anarchism is. Most anarchists reject terrorism for nationalist or religious purposes, but in a theoretical sense, anarchism justifies terrorism as a form of criminal action that attacks the values of an organised, complacent society. Anarchism is a theory of governance that rejects any form of central or external authority, preferring instead to replace it with alternative forms of organisation such as shaming rituals for deviants, mutual assistance pacts between citizens, syndicalism (any non-authoritarian organisational structure that gives the greatest freedom to workers), iconoclasm (the destruction of cherished beliefs), libertarianism (a belief in absolute liberty), and plain old rugged individualism. Anarchism is often referred to as the nineteenth century roots of terrorism, the term first being introduced in 1840 by Pierre-Joseph Proudhon. Anarchism defined as the rejection of the state, of any form of coercive government, of any form of domination and exploitation. It is the notion of free and equal access to all the world's resources to enable positive freedom in place of negative freedom.[2]

As a theory, anarchism holds a unique place in history because it was the first revolutionary movement to come up with systematic ideas about the purpose of agitation. Major anarchist figures, like Karl Heinzen and Johann Most, contributed the idea that murder, especially murder-suicide, constituted the highest form of revolutionary struggle. Both advocated the use of weapons of mass destruction. Other anarchists contributed different ideas, such as Peter Kropotkin's notion of "propaganda by word" or radicalising the public by use of subversive publications. Minor figures in the history of anarchism, like Charles Gallo, Auguste Vaillante, Emile Henry, and Claudius Konigstein advocated the idea that to have the most effect, the targets must be innocents (in places such as crowded dance halls or shopping centers) or symbols of economic success (like banks and stock exchanges). Between 1875 and 1912, anarchists alone or in small groups managed to assassinate or attempt to assassinate the leaders of nine (9) different countries, including the US (with President William McKinley in 1901). These crimes were just the most well-known acts of anarchism, as anarchists were involved in numerous ordinary crimes such as theft, robbery, murder, kidnapping, assault, and bombing. The most famous incident was the Haymarket riot in Chicago during 1886. During these peak years for classic anarchism, May Day celebrations became famous as all-out crime-rampant days. Police departments around the world became convinced there was an international conspiracy, and suspicious foreigners were locked up by the hundreds in many countries. Perfunctory trials were held, and many defendants were hanged or deported.[3]

Classic anarchism started to break up during the Russian

Revolution, when something called anarcho-communism (also called libertarian communism) came about. Peter Kropotkin is generally regarded as the most important theorist of this strand, but charismatic figures in the 1920s such as Nestor Makhno were just as important. Anarcho-communism (as opposed to collectivist anarchism) totally rejects the idea of ownership in favour of the idea of usage. They also believe in spontaneous satisfaction of bodily needs and urges. Twentieth-century terrorist groups which later claimed an ancestry with anarchism includes: the Japanese Red Army, the British Angry Brigade, the German Baader-Meinh of Gang, the Weatherman in the United States, and the Mexican Zapatista movement (Kushner 2003). However, the theory of anarchism of terrorism has mostly died out, because, most anarchist have accepted organised movement as a method of protest. Modern anarchism does not support terrorism, and there is a weak theoretical link between the two.[4]

(ii) Theory of Fascism

The word comes from the Latin "fasces" which means 'to use power to scare or impress people'. It generally refers to the consolidation of all economic and political power into some form of super-patriotism that is devoted to genocide or endless war with one's enemies. Benito Mussolini, who practically invented the term in 1922, said it is the merger of state and corporate power. Mussolini's version of fascism was based on the idea of an indomitable power and an attempt to resurrect imperial Rome. Adolf Hitler said fascism is the clever and constant application of propaganda so that people can be made to see paradise as hell, and the other way around. Fascism supports terrorism at home and abroad. Charismatic leaders are usually given supreme powers to crack down on dissidents, peace-makers, and anyone who doesn't abide by the "cult of the individual" which worships a He-man mentality and the party line. With the frequent wars and militaristic ventures that come with fascism, an effort is made to demonise the enemy as sub-humans, who deserve extinction. These enemies are also made into scapegoats for all the past problems a country has had.[5]

Frustrated fascists, who fail to gain control in their own countries have historically turned to terrorism. They are most likely to turn to domestic terrorism since fascists do not believe that citizen rights are bestowed merely because someone inhabits a country. Nor do they believe that all human beings are possessed of equal rights; they are particularly violent against foreign families and corporations, which have been accused of poisoning the family and property relations. Fascism is full of ironies and contradictions. On the one hand, it is anti-modern in its glorification of the land, a return to country life, and its fascination with peasant dress or costume. On the other hand, it is pro-modern in its worship of military technology, favouritism of big business, mass mobilisation of people, promotion of commercialised sport, and its surprisingly liberal attitude toward the involvement of women in the movement. Just as anarchists have their May Day (May 1st) celebrations, fascists also tend to celebrate anniversaries. Many terrorists, of course, have been known to time their attacks to coincide with the date for an historical event or the birthday of someone special to them.[6]

(iii) Philosophical Theory of Religion

A number of criminologists have pointed out that the disciplines of theology, religion, and philosophy have had important things to say about terrorism. They point to the fact that about a quarter of all terrorist groups and about half of the most dangerous ones on earth are primarily motivated by religious concerns. They believe that God not only approves of their action, but that God demands their action. Religious terrorism is not about extremism, fanaticism, sects, or cults, but is instead all about a fundamentalist or militant interpretation of the basic tenets. The trick to successful use of terrorism in the name of religion rests upon convincing believers or converters that a "neglected duty" exists in the fundamental, mainstream part of the religion. Most religious traditions are filled with plenty of violent images at their core, and destruction or self-destruction is a central part of the logic behind religion-based terrorism. Terrorism as an outcome of religious fanaticism mostly arises with the emergence of a charismatic leader, who blames the State functionaries, and global trends like secularism, modernity and westernisation for their perceived neglect. The strength of fundamentalism is its ability to guarantee a radical change without specifying exactly what it will look like. However, once a semi-vague enemy has been identified, the religious movement borrows the idea of "sovereignty" from the political realm and begins to see itself as the legitimate defender of the faith and legitimate restorer of dignity to the homeland. Perhaps the most interesting aspect of religion as a theory of terrorism is how a devout believer could come to mix politics and religion in such a way. The answer is in the conception of worship that may help to discover the true nature of God. Despite being an important cause of terrorism, it must still be maintained with all fairness that most militant religious groups only adopt terrorism as a tactic of last resort.[7]

(iv) Economics Theory of Rational Choice

The discipline of economics has many concepts that are relevant to an understanding of terrorism – supply and demand, costs and benefits, etc. Fully-developed economic or econometric models of terrorism are quite rare, however, and often involve such things as "psychic" costs and benefits. Rational choice theory, in particular, has found a place in criminology, and holds that people will engage in crime after weighing the costs and benefits of their actions to arrive at a rational choice about motivation after perceiving that the chances of gain outweigh any possible punishment or loss. According to this theory, terrorism is not a pathological phenomenon and the resort to terrorism is not an aberration. The central focus of study ought to be on why some groups find terrorism useful, and in standard control theory fashion, why other groups do not find terrorism useful. Some groups may continue to work with established patterns of dissident action. Other groups may resort to terrorism because they have tried other alternatives. Factors that influence the rational choice of terrorism include place, size, time, and the climate of international opinion. A terrorist plot in a democratic society is less likely to involve senseless violence than a scheme hatched under an authoritarian regime because under the latter, terrorists realise they have nothing to lose with the expected repercussions.[8]

(v) Theory of Globalisation

According to this theory, globalisation has created the structures and institutions, which fuel terrorist movements. Globalisation is the term used to describe the current economic order where all nations share a global market and enjoy the equal opportunities to reap the fruits of free trade. However, the decades of globalisation has produced one of the greatest disparities in the economic conditions of the countries of the world. Globalisation has fuelled explosive patterns of social polarisation within and between nations, and this has been accepted as a cause of terrorism. Globalisation theory is further tied into ideas about colonialism, imperialism, and neo-colonialism. The first two words are often used interchangeably to describe a set of conditions where the mores, values, and beliefs of the colonisers are considered superior to those of the colonised. However, when the assumption is made that (imperial) power is a necessary thing to maintain cultural superiority; this is the usual meaning of imperialism.[9]

(vi) Sociological Theories

Modern sociological perspectives are primarily concerned with the social construction of fear or panic, and how institutions and processes, especially the media, primary and secondary groups, maintain that expression of fear. Regardless of the name for the theoretical viewpoint, one is likely to encounter the following, or some variation of them, as causal factors in almost all etiological, sociology-related thinking –

(a) the frustration-aggression hypothesis,

(b) the relative deprivation hypothesis,

(c) the negative identity hypothesis,

(d) the narcissistic rage hypothesis, and

(e) the moral disengagement hypothesis

The frustration-aggression hypothesis is the idea that every frustration (not being able to engage in some behaviour) leads to some form of aggression, and that every aggressive act relieves that frustration to some extent. The relative deprivation hypothesis is the idea that as a person goes about choosing their values and interests; they compare what they have and don't have, as well as what they want or don't want, with real or imaginary others. The negative identity hypothesis is the idea that, for whatever reason, a person develops a vindictive and covert rejection of the roles and statuses laid out for them by their family, community, or society. The narcissistic rage hypothesis is an umbrella idea for all the numerous things that can go wrong in child-rearing, such as too much smothering, too little smothering, ineffective discipline, overly stringent discipline, psychological trauma, coming from a broken home, etc., that all leads to the same effect of a "What about Me?" reaction in the child. The moral disengagement hypothesis is the idea that encompasses all the way a person neutralises or removes any inhibitions they have about committing acts of horrific violence. Some common patterns include imagining one's self as a hero, portraying one's self as a functionary, minimising the harm done, dehumanising the victim, or insulating one's self in routine activities.[10]

(vii) Psychological Theory of Terrorism

Although most psychologists refuse to accept the existence of the concept of 'terrorist personality,' it is mostly accepted that terrorists typically suffer from low self-esteem, are attracted to groups with charismatic leaders, and enjoy risk-taking. According to psychological theory, most terrorists feel that they are doing nothing wrong when they kill and injure people. They seem to share a feature of the psychological condition known as anti-social personality disorder or psychopathic personality disorder, which is reflected by an absence of empathy for the suffering of others. However, they do not appear unstable or mentally ill for this. A common feature is a type of thinking such as "I am good and right. You are bad and wrong." It is a very polarised thinking which allows them to distance themselves from opponents and makes it easier for them to kill people. According to both the sociological and the psychological theories, individuals join terrorist organisations in order to commit acts of terrorism, and that this process is the same as when individuals join criminal sub-cultures in order to commit acts of crime. There appears to be no unique terrorist personality. Instead, there appear to be unique sub-cultural phenomena which develop, support, and enhance a penchant for cold-blooded, calculated violence which, if not satisfied within a terrorist organisation might be fulfilled elsewhere. Terrorism is a social activity. Individuals join a terrorist group usually after they have tried other forms of political involvement. The emotional links between individuals and the strength of commitment to their ideology appear to become stronger by the group living in the underground and facing adversity in the form of counter-terrorism.[11]

(viii) Biological Theories

David Hubbard (1983), was one of the first biological researchers of terrorism, and his line of work is similar to the familiar cycle of violence hypothesis in criminal justice. According to him, people who commit repetitive and cyclical acts of violence (which would include wife beaters, rapists, and serial killers) are driven by hormonal or neuro-chemical fluctuations in their body or brain chemistry. Three compounds, in particular, have been singled out as having abnormal levels among terrorists: nor epinephrine, acetylcholine, and endorphins. Of these, nor epinephrine is suspected as being the most influential, as it is associated with the so-called flight or fight mechanism in human biology. The theory of "fight or flight" was developed by W.B. Cannon back in 1929, and refers to a state of arousal under stress in which the heart, lungs, and muscle operate more efficiently. As it applies to terrorism, the behavioural requirements of such activities (fighting exhilaration before an event, and fleeing manipulation of audience after an event) produce a syndrome of physiological need for arousal at fairly regular intervals. Motives for terrorism appear to be quite stable when the biological view point is taken, and it is possible to link a variety of aspects in the typical terrorist profile with biological factors. For example, xenophobia may be biological induced since the fear of strangers tends to be discernible even at infantile stages of development. Other explanations might involve insights from sociobiology or kin selection theory in evolutionary psychology.[12]

Kinds of Terrorism

Terrorists are motivated by different goals and objectives. Depending on the objectives the nature of terrorism also differs. Terrorism may be of many kinds. Terrorism may be classified on the following categories:

(i) International, National and Regional Terrorism

Terrorism may be international, national or regional. International terrorism is any act of terror-violence containing an international element e.g., the perpetrator may be from one state while the victim belongs to another state, or the terrorist act may in a jurisdiction foreign to both. In short, when the sphere of application of any terrorism transcends the boundary of a nation-State, it is called international terrorism.

The terrorism perpetrated by the Liberation Tigers of Tamil Elam (LTTE) and Khalistanis are regional in character, as these are restricted to a particular region of a nation-State. The LTTE wants to form a separate Tamil State (Tamil Elam) in the northern part of Sri Lanka. The Khalistanis wanted to make the Punjab province of India a separate Sate of Khalistan. The terrorism adopted by the Palestine Liberation Organisation (PLO) is national. Their aim is to establish a Palestine State is Palestine. The Irish Republic Army (IRA) also may be called national. They want to reunify Ireland.[13]

(ii) Domestic Terrorism

Domestic terrorism is harder to define than international terrorism because domestic terrorism is usually included in state criminal statutes under acts committed by common criminals. Some states define terrorism as a crime, others define it as an act of war, and most states consider terrorism to be a method used to commit other more specifically defined crimes against the person or against property. International terrorism, like domestic terrorism, is a method used to perpetrate other crimes, and as such international terrorism is arguably included under the category of other international crimes but only if the five necessary structural elements of terrorism are present. Thus, international terrorism is an elusive concept that overlaps with other international crimes but which can be included in the definitions of these other crimes, if the five necessary elements are present, like the intentional use or threat of violence for political, religious or ideological purposes resulting in the harm of innocent civilians.

(iii) State Sponsored Terrorism and Terrorism against the State

Depending on who is terrorising whom, terrorism may be classified into state-sponsored terrorism and terrorism against the state. As the name itself suggests, state-sponsored terrorism is 'sponsored' by one State against another State, though the degree of sponsorship may vary from case to case. State sponsored terrorism is also committed when a sponsoring State directly controls terrorist activities aimed at the enemy state. The struggles organised against the unjust British Rule in India by Indian revolutionaries like Khudiram, Binoy-Badal-Dinesh, Bhagat Singh was terrorism against the State. On the other hand, the repression by Hitler, Mussolini and Stalin were glaring examples of state sponsored terrorism. The planned killing of Palestinian people by Israeli armed forces is also terrorism by a state. The case may be further extended to include terrorism by a stronger state against a weaker state, and terrorism by a group of weaker state against stronger state. The stronger state may use terrorism to overawe the weaker states, or compelled them to be subservient to its own interest. The USA's attack on Afghanistan and Iraq and threat to Syria are acts of terrorism by a stronger state against a weaker counterpart. On the other hand the 11th September, 2001 attacks on the WTC and Pentagon were acts of terrorism against a stronger state allegedly by a group (Al-Qaeda) by a weaker state.

The question on defining terrorism is whether States can commit terrorism, or whether terrorists are only non-State actors (such as individuals or organised armed groups). According to many scholars and experts, it is unnecessary to include government conduct in the definition of terrorism, as the existing areas of international law – such as human rights, humanitarian law, international criminal law, the law on the use of force, the law of State responsibility, and the law of the United Nations Charter etc., – already clarified what States can and cannot do. In their view, a legal definition of terrorism is necessary precisely because the violent activities of non-State actors are not fully covered by these international laws, which principally impose obligations on States. On the other hand, some scholars and experts have argued that terror inflicted by States is far more dangerous and prevalent than non-State terror, such as the bombing and killing of civilians by armed forces in war, large scale oppression and intimidation of civilian populations by their own governments etc. Existing international law is not considered sufficient to control and restrain such violence by States, which has continued unabated despite legal controls. In addition, because the term 'terrorism' is morally powerful in condemning and stigmatising those to whom it is applied, the term should be equally applied to States and non-State actors if they commit equivalent conduct – terrifying civilians for political ends.

However, all the treaties and conventions relating to terrorism are discriminatory in that they conclude that terrorist activities can be committed only by non-state actors and, conversely, that state actors can never be terrorists or that a state will never employ terror for its political benefit. For example, the 1997 Bombings Convention identifies terrorism on the basis of the means used [Article 1(3)], and the place of occurrence [Article 2(1)], but its preamble clearly provides that states are not covered under this convention but are covered under international humanitarian law.

It is unfortunate that terrorism is being committed by the state for achieving its own aims in spite of its prohibition. It is so mainly because international law regarding the implementation and enforcement of its rules is not as strong as it should be. Its weaknesses have resulted in committing the terrorism by states especially by those which are enormous and powerful. It has become a part of the system and as a weapon of warfare used by a government against another government. If states are at all serious to curb terrorism, they themselves have to realise that the immoral and inhuman act of terrorism brings sufferings and miseries to human beings. Its elimination therefore depends primarily upon the political will of the states.[14]

All forms of state involvement in terrorism are usually placed under the general category of 'state sponsored terrorism.' Depending upon the state involvement in terrorist attacks following classification of states can be made according to their level of involvement in terrorism[15] –

(i) *States supporting terrorism:* States that support terrorist organisations, providing financial aid, and ideological support, military or operational assistance.

(ii) *States operating terrorism:* States that initiate, direct and perform terrorist activities through groups outside their own institutions.

(iii) *States perpetrating terrorism*: States perpetrating terrorist acts abroad through their own official bodies – members of its security forces or its intelligence services, or their direct agents. In other words, states intentionally attacking civilians in other countries in order to achieve political aims without declaring war.

State sponsorship of terrorism in the territory of another state is specifically forbidden by the UN General Assembly's '*Declaration of Principles of International Law*'.[16] The principles established by the General Assembly in the *Friendly Relations Declaration of 1970,* proclaiming the duty of every state to refrain from organising, instigating, assisting or participating in terrorist acts in another state or acquiescing in organised activities within its territory directed towards the commission of such acts, have also been reiterated by the Security Council in its *resolution 1189* (1998).[17] A different situation arises where a State supports the activities in another State of a terrorist or militant group determined to undermine the territorial integrity of the latter State or overthrow the existing government of the latter State. In the *Nicaragua* case,[18] the ICJ considered the relevant principles for determining the responsibility of the former State in such situations and laid down the 'control and dependency' test for this purpose. According to this test, 'merely' financing, organising, training, supplying and equipping the rebel group is not enough to establish the responsibility of the Doer State. For this conduct to give rise to legal responsibility of the Doer State, 'it would in principle have to be proved that State had effective control of the military or paramilitary operations in the course of which the alleged violations were committed.'

(iv) Religious Terrorism

Present day terrorist activities around the world are motivated largely by religious imperatives. The practitioners of terrorism motivated either in whole or in part by a religious imperative consider violence as a divine duty or a sacramental act. It embraces different means of legitimisation and justification compared to other terrorist groups, and these distinguishing factors make religious terrorism more destructive in nature. Religious terrorism can be initiated by both a minority and a majority religion or sect of a nation. Catholic-Protestant violence in Ireland is an example of religious terrorism. Both al-Fatah and Hamas struggle for the liberation of Palestine. The majority of both the organisations are Muslims. But the former uses terrorism in the name of secular nationalism, but the latter does it in the name of religion. Similarly, terrorism by the Stern Gang and Irgun Zvai Leaumi of Palestine and Jewish Defence League of USA, who are fighting for the Zionist cause, are Jewish religious terrorist organisations. Again, the Christian Patriots Defence League, the Covenant, the Sword and the Arm of the Lord, the Order, Pose Comitatus and the Skinheads of the USA fight for the Christian cause and so are Christian religious terrorist organisations.

(v) Ideology-oriented Terrorism

Any ideology can be used to support the use of violence and terrorism. Ideology-oriented terrorism is generally classified into two: Left-wing and Right-wing terrorism.

(a) Left-wing Terrorism:

Violence against the ruling elite mostly by the peasant class motivated by what is called Leftist ideologies have occurred time and again in history. However, a concrete ideological base for the Left and subsequent violent movements was inspired by the writings of Marx and Engels. This was supported by the writings and speeches of later Communists like Lenin and Mao Tse-tung (Mao Zedong). Leftist ideologies believe that all the existing social relations and state structures in the capitalist society are exploitative in character and a revolutionary change through violent means is essential. Examples of Leftist ideologies that have resorted to the use of terror are numerous. These include; the Red Army Faction or Baader Meinhof Gang in the former West Germany, the Red Brigades in Italy, the 17th November Movement in Greece, the Shining Path of Peru, People's Revolutionary Army and the Motoneros of Argentina and the Maoist groups in India and Nepal are the most easily identifiable groups' closer home.[19]

(b) Right-wing Terrorism:

Right-wing groups generally seek to maintain the status-quo or to return to some past situation that they feel should have been conserved. Sometimes groups espousing rightist ideologies might assume ethnic/racist character too. They may force the government to acquire a territory or to intervene to protect the rights of an 'oppressed' minority in a neighboring country, (i.e., the Nazi Party in Germany). Violence against migrant communities also comes under this category of terrorist violence. Examples of these are: Nazism in Germany, Fascists in Italy, white supremacy movements in the US known as Ku Klux Klan (KKK), the Green Jackets of Denmark in the 1980s etc.[20]

(vi) Bio-terrorism

Bio-terrorism refers to the intentional release of toxic biological agents to harm and terrorise civilians, in the name of a political or other cause. A bio-terrorism attack is the deliberate release of viruses, bacteria, or other germs (agents) used to cause illness or death in people, animals, or plants. These agents are typically found in nature, but it is possible that they could be changed to increase their ability to cause disease, make them resistant to current medicines, or to increase their ability to be spread into the environment. Biological agents can be spread through the air, through water, or in food. Terrorists may use biological agents because they can be extremely difficult to detect and do not cause illness for several hours to several days. Some bio-terrorism agents, like the small pox virus, can be spread from person to person and some, like anthrax, cannot.[21]

The fear of the unknown and unseen biological weapons may create silent terror in a populous community. Awareness, education and training are only defence modes against new and emerging diseases of bio-terrorism. Historical findings reveal that France was the first country to use bacteria as biological weapons to thin out army and disorganise the transport of draft animals for war purpose in the late 1930s and later various States began biological warfare activities as part of offensive and defensive programmes. The biological weapons, pathogenic micro-organisms, which release certain poisonous toxins, lethal at very low concentration, are the most potential source of bio-terrorism and are a real threat to the security of public health and international peace. Some potential typical examples of biological warfare agents are anthrax, botulism, plagues and small pox. Bio-terrorism is considered to be another easy accessible form of asymmetric warfare adopted by the terrorist forces. Industry, buildings, water supplies and agriculture are more vulnerable and potential threats for crippling the economy, creating instability, terrorising the masses psychologically, causing deaths and ill-effects on living systems and can spread through different routes.[22]

Firstly, to tackle this, the first and the foremost is educating the masses about the strategies and resources available to cope with any kind of eventuality.

Secondly, strengthening of emergency response capabilities, identification of hospitals, notifying the affected areas and good communication system would help.

Thirdly, net-working of different agencies, involving in the community safety and nation's security.

Fourthly, understanding of human physiology and enhancing the funding for research on molecular biological studies.

Fifthly, evolving effective management policy.[23]

(vii) Chemical, Radiological and Nuclear Terrorism

Nowadays, chemical, radiological and nuclear terrorism is also causing massive death and destruction to the people and society at large. Radiological and nuclear terrorism is widely considered as a major if not the ultimate terrorist threat for modern societies. Highly industrialised countries could be extremely sensitive to terrorist aggressions of this kind. Nuclear terrorism is often associated with nuclear proliferation. Strictly speaking, nuclear proliferation deals with the spread of nuclear weapons into states which doesn't possess them. But proliferation can also be understood as the spread of radioactive material or even nuclear explosives into the hands of non-state organisations, such as sub-national terrorist or criminal organisations as well as any kind of extremist groups for sabotage, blackmail or any other destabilisation or destruction purposes.[24] Nuclear terrorism means terrorism whose primary means is explosion by nuclear fission or fusion, or reasonably educated attempts at such Nuclear terrorism refers to a number of different ways nuclear materials might be exploited as a terrorist tactic. These include attacking nuclear facilities, purchasing nuclear weapons, or building nuclear weapons or otherwise finding ways to disperse radioactive materials.

The *International Convention for the Suppression of Acts of Nuclear Terrorism, 2005*[25] (Nuclear Terrorism Convention) details offences relating to unlawful and intentional possession and use of radioactive material or a radioactive device, and use or damage of nuclear facilities. It is designed to promote co-operation among countries through the sharing of information and the providing of assistance for investigations and extraditions. According to this Convention, 'Radioactive material' means nuclear material and other radioactive substances which contain nuclides which undergo spontaneous disintegration (a process accompanied by emission of one or more types of ionising radiation, such as *alpha, beta, neutron* particles and *gamma* rays) and which may, owing to their radiological or fissile properties, cause death, serious bodily injury or substantial damage to property or to the environment. According to this Convention "Nuclear material" means plutonium, except that with isotopic concentration exceeding 80 per cent in plutonium -238; uranium-233; uranium enriched in the isotope 235 or 233; uranium containing the mixture of isotopes as occurring in nature other than in the form of ore or ore residue; or any material containing one or more of the foregoing; Whereby "uranium enriched in the isotope 235 or 233" means uranium containing the isotope 235 or 233 or both in an amount such that the abundance ratio of the sum of these isotopes to the isotope 238 is greater than the ratio of the isotope 235 to the isotope 238 occurring in nature.[26]

In 1972, members of the Order of the Rising Sun in the United States possessed 30-40 kilograms of typhoid bacteria cultures for use against water supplies in major Mid-west cities. In 1980, police in Paris discovered a biological laboratory with clostridium botulinum culture belonging to the German Baader-Meinhof Gang. In 1986, typhoid (salmonella typhus) was used by the Rajneesh religious cult in Oregon to contaminate salad bars in restaurants, resulting in 750 case of food poisoning. On 20th March, 1995, the first major use of chemical weapons by terrorists occurred. Members of Japanese radical cult, Aum Shinrikyo, placed containers of the deadly chemical nerve agent (sarin) on five trains of the Tokyo sub-way system. The cultists then punctured the containers and released poisonous gas into the trains and sub-way stations. While the attack resulted in the death of 12 persons, 5500 others were injured. In sum, biological and chemical weapons have many advantages for terrorists. These benefits include their low cost, and the ease and speed of their production; further, they can be developed by individuals with a limited education and facilities.

Development of nuclear weapons began in the 1940s. In 1941, the British began a nuclear weapons' research program. Fearing German production of nuclear weapons during World War-II, the United States and allied nations joined efforts and the Manhattan Project began. In 1945, the United States dropped an atomic bomb on Hiroshima, Japan, and created the world's first radiologic public health emergency, resulting in 60,000-70,000 immediate deaths. When this failed to persuade the Japanese to surrender, the United States dropped a second bomb on Nagasaki, Japan, three days later, resulting in another 40,000 deaths. Within five years, anestimated 340,000 Japanese, mostly civilians, had died as a result of the two bombs. In 1949, the Cold War began with the Soviet Union's first nuclear test. The United Kingdom, France, and China also joined the United States in nuclear weapons' testing. Since 1949, approximately 2,000 nuclear test explosions have taken place around the world. More recently, threats of radiologic terrorism from Al-Qaeda were raised in 2002 when 31-year-old Jose Padilla was detained on suspicion that he intended to deploy a radiologic dispersal device (RDD) in the United States; detailed plans for RDDs were uncovered after the destruction of an al-Qaeda training camp in Afghanistan.[27]

Radiologic terrorism events include, for example, radiation sources intentionally hidden in public places (sometimes referred to as "radiologic exposure devices" or REDs); RDDs; attacks on nuclear facilities or radioactive materials in transit on trucks and trains that result in intentional release of radioactive materials; and detonation of malfunctioning nuclear weapons that result in no nuclear yield. The most common type of RDD is the "dirty bomb"; this type of RDD employs conventional explosives to disperse radioactive materials. Other RDD dispersal methods may include techniques such as an aerosol or spray.[28]

Nuclear events involve the use of nuclear weapons, devices that use fission or fusion reactions to produce destructive energy in pulses or waves of heat, electro-magnetic energy, air pressure, and radiation. Nuclear weapons are described by their potential yield or the energy released in their detonation, measured in kilotons (kT). A 1-kT nuclear device, for example, refers to the approximate equivalent explosive yield from one metric tonne of the chemical explosive trinitrotoluene. Weapons that are capable of producing 0.01–10 kT are considered low yield. For several reasons, including the high-level security of intact high-yield weapons and extreme sophistication needed to construct high-yield weapons, low-yield weapons are considered much more likely to be used by terrorist organisations. Although these weapons are called low yield, even the lowest-yield weapon, 0.01 kT, would have an explosive impact greater than the Oklahoma City bombing in 1995. The nuclear weapons detonated at Hiroshima and Nagasaki had a yield of 15 and 21 kT, respectively.[29]

(viii) Narco-terrorism

The term 'narco-terrorism' was first used by the former President of Peru, Belaunde Terry in 1983 to describe campaigns by drug-traffickers using terrorist methods such as the use of car bombs, assassinations and kidnapping against the anti-narcotics police in Coloumbia and Peru. Though, initially used in the context of drug-trafficking related terrorism in South America, the term has come to be associated with terrorist groups and activities around the world and more so in the Central and South-east Asia. Narco-terrorism has been defined as 'the attempt by narcotics traffickers to influence the policies of the government by systematic threat or use by violence'. However, it is also possible to view narco-terrorism as a means of terrorism or at any rate as a means of funding terrorism. As the term itself suggests, narco-terrorism combines two criminal activities; drug-trafficking and terrorist violence. Narco-terrorism is motivated mainly by economic reasons as it helps the terrorist organisations raise huge sums of money with minimum cost for their activities. Thus, the political, ideological, religious and the ethno-nationalist motives generally associated with terrorism are secondary to the economic gains associated with it.[30]

In a survey conducted by the United Nations, links between drug-traffickers and terrorist groups were observed in 19 out of 38 countries. These countries include Algeria, Colombia, Comoros, Ecuador, Germany, Guernsey, India, Italy, Japan, Kenya, Kyrgyzstan, Lithuania, Mauritius, Saudi Arabia, Turkey, the United Kingdom, the

United States of America, Uzbekistan and Yemen. Major terrorist groups operating on these lines in these countries are: Al-Qaeda, the Colombia-based AUC (United Defences of Columbia), ELN (National Liberation Army), Colombia, and FARC (Revolutionary Armed Forces of Colombia), the tri-border Islamic Group in Argentina, Paraguay and Brazil, the Shining Path in Peru, the PKK (Kurdistan Workers Party) in Turkey, IMU (Islamic Movement of Uzbekistan) in Uzbekistan, the Islamic Jihad in Palestine, Hizbollah in Lebanon, and the RIRA (Real Irish Republican Army) in Northern Ireland. Islamist terrorist groups in India supported by the Pakistan ISI are reported to be active in drug-trafficking along the Kashmir Valley and also in other parts of the country.[31]

(ix) Cyber Terrorism

The term Cyber Terrorism is becoming increasingly common nowadays, yet a solid definition for it and what it constitutes is subjective and covers a wide area. Information technology (IT) has exposed the user to a huge data bank of information regarding everything and anything. However, it has also added a new dimension to terrorism. Recent reports suggest that the terrorist is also getting equipped to utilise cyber space to carryout terrorist attacks. Terrorism related to cyber is popularly known as 'cyber terrorism.' In the 1980s, Barry Collin, a senior research fellow at the Institute for Security and Intelligence in California, coined the term "cyber terrorism" to refer to the convergence of cyberspace and terrorism.[32]

Cyber terrorism is the convergence of terrorism and cyber space. It is generally understood to mean unlawful attacks and threats of attacks against computers, networks, and information stored therein when done to intimidate or coerce a government or its people in furtherance of political or social objectives, Further, to qualify as cyber terrorism, an attack should result in violence against persons or property or at least cause enough harm to generate fear. Attacks that lead to death or bodily injury, explosions, plane crashes, water contamination or severe economic loss would be examples. Serious attacks against critical infrastructures could be acts of cyber terrorism depending upon their impact. The US (FBI) defines cyber terrorism as; any premeditated, politically motivated attack against information, computer systems, computer programs, and data which results in violence against non-combatant objectives by sub-national groups or clandestine agents.[33]

There is a representative definition of cyber-terrorism proposed by *National Infrastructure Protection Center* (NIPC) that cyber-terrorism is a criminal act perpetrated by the use of computers and telecommunications capabilities, resulting in violence, destruction and or disruption of services to create fear by causing confusion and uncertainty within a given population, with the objective of influencing a government to conform to a particular political, social, or ideological agenda.[34]

Cyber terrorism is one kind of cyber attack. Too often the terms cyber terrorism and cyber attack are used interchangeably and may result in a misunderstanding of the cyber threat in g‑neral and the threat of cyber terrorism in particular. These definitions demonstrate that for cyber terrorism to be perpetrated there are at least three elements which must be satisfied in order to distinguish a cyber terrorist attack from an ordinary cyber attack. Denning notes that politically motivated cyber attacks that lead to death or bodily injury, explosions, or severe economic loss would be examples of cyber terrorism. Serious attacks against critical infrastructures could be acts of cyber terrorism, depending on their impact. Attacks that disrupt non-essential services or that are mainly a costly nuisance would not.

Cyber terrorism can be the use of computing assets to threaten or force others. An example of cyber terrorism could be hacking into a hospital computer system and changing someone's medicine prescription to a lethal dosage as an act of revenge. It sounds farfetched, but these things can and do happen. Cyber terrorism has also been defined as "the use of computing resources against persons or property to intimidate or coerce a government, the civilian population, or any segment thereof, in furtherance of political or social objectives."[35]

There are many forms of terrorism on the Internet. Some are not dangerous enough to be deemed a simple spread of information instead of terrorism. They are simple show of skill and are harmless. Acts of cyber crimes may involve stealing of money, company secrets, or attacking country's infrastructure and causing real damage. By using the Internet, the terrorist can influence much wider harm or change to a country than one could by killing some people. From immobilising a countries military defence to shutting off the power in a large area, the terrorist can have an effect on more people at less danger to him or herself, than through other means. Cyber terrorism takes many forms; some examples of cyber-terrorism are given below[36].

First, Cyber-terrorists often commit acts of terrorism purely for private gain. Such a group, known as the Chaos Computer Club, was exposed in 1997. They had formed an Active-X Control for the account. Without difficulty, this could be used to steal money from users all over the world that have the Quicken software installed on their computer. This type of file is only one of thousands of types of viruses that can do everything from simply annoy users, to disable large networks, which can have disastrous, even life and death, results.

Secondly, Cyber terrorist is interested in gaining publicity in any probable way. For example, information warfare procedures like Trojan horse viruses and network worms are repeatedly used to not only do harm to computing resources, but also as a way for the designer of the viruses to "brag." This is a serious moral issue because many people are affected by these cases. The viruses can use system resources until networks become ineffective, costing companies' lots of time and money. In addition, depending on the type of work done on the affected computers, the damage to the recipients of that work could be lethal; it could have unpredictable effects that could have dreadful consequences.

In 1998, Spanish protestors bombarded the Institute for Global Communications (IGC) with thousands of bogus e-mail messages. E-mail was tied up and undeliverable to the ISP's users, and support lines were tied up with people who couldn't get their mail. The protestors also spammed IGC staff and member accounts, clogged their Web page with bogus credit card orders, and threatened to employ the same tactics against organisations using IGC services. They demanded that IGC stop hosting the web-site for the Euskal Herria Journal, a New York-based publication supporting Basque independence. Protestors said IGC supported terrorism because a section on the Web pages contained materials on the terrorist group ETA, which claimed responsibility for assassinations of Spanish political and security officials, and attacks on military installations. IGC finally relented and pulled the site because of the "mail bombings." This is an act of cyber terrorism. The normal activities of the ISP in cyber space have been disrupted by using a preplanned methodology and the intention of the attackers is to further a political objective.

In 1998, ethnic Tamil guerrillas swamped Sri Lankan embassies with 800 e-mails a day over a two-week period. The messages read, "We are the Internet Black Tigers and we're doing this to disrupt your communications." Intelligence authorities characterised it as the first known attack by terrorists against a country's computer systems.

Since December 1997, the Electronic Disturbance Theater (EDT) has been conducting Web sit-ins against various sites in support of the Mexican Zapatistas. At a designated time, thousands of protestors point their browsers to a target site using software that floods the target with rapid and repeated download requests. EDT's software has also been used by animal rights groups against organisations said to abuse animals. Electro hippies, another group of hacktivists, conducted Web sit-ins against the WTO when they met in Seattle in late 1999.

During the Kosovo conflict in 1999, hackers attacked NATO computers. The computers flooded them with e-mail and hit them with a denial of service (DoS). The hackers were protesting against the NATO bombings of the Chinese embassy in Belgrade. Businesses, public organisations and academic institutions were bombarded with highly politicised e-mails containing viruses from other Eastern European countries, according to reports.

In February, 2000, a blizzard of attacks disabled some of the most popular web-sites, among them CNN, e-Bay, Yahoo, Amazon.com and E-Trade. These attacks known as denial of service (DoS) attacks flooded the networks with fake messages that prevented legitimate traffic from flowing.

Recently, in May 2007 Estonia was subjected to a mass cyber-attack in the wake of the removal of a Russian World War-II war memorial from downtown Tallinn. The attack was a distributed denial-of-service attack in which selected sites were bombarded with traffic to force them offline; nearly all Estonian government ministry networks as well as two major Estonian bank networks were knocked offline; in addition, the political party website of Estonia's current Prime

Minister Andrus Ansip featured a counterfeit letter of apology from Ansip for removing the memorial statue. Despite speculation that the attack had been co-ordinated by the Russian government, Estonia's defence minister admitted he had no conclusive evidence linking cyber attacks to Russian authorities. Russia called accusations of its involvement "unfounded," and neither NATO nor European Commission experts were able to find any conclusive proof of official Russian government participation.

References

1. O'Connor, T.R. (2009). The Criminology of Terrorism: Theories and Models. In K. Borgeson, and R. Valeri (Eds.), *Terrorism in America*, (pp. 17-42). Burlington: Jones and Bartlett Publishers, 2009.
2. *Ibid.*
3. *Ibid.*
4. *Ibid.*
5. *Ibid.*
6. *Ibid.*
7. *Ibid.*
8. *Ibid.*
9. *Ibid.*
10. *Ibid.*
11. *Ibid.*
12. *Ibid.*
13. Islam, N. (2005). *Islam 9/11 and Global Terrorism: A Study of Perception and Solutions*, (pp. 9-15), New Delhi: Viva Books Private Limited.
14. Agarwal, Dr. H.O. (2006). *International Terrorism' in International Law and Human Rights* (p. 625). Faridabad: Allahabad Law Agency.
15. Gonar, B. (2002). Defining Terrorism: Is one Man's Terrorist Another Man's Freedom Fighter?, *Media Asia – An Asian*

Mass Communication Quarterly, 29(3), Singapore. pp. 123-133.

16. *Declaration on Principles of International Law Concerning Friendly Relations and Co-operation among States in accordance with the Charter of the United Nations,* GA. Res. 2625 (XXV) of 24 Oct. 1970 UNGAOR, 25th Sess. Supp. 28, p. 121, U.N. Doc A/8028(1971). Retrieved January 05, 2012 from http://daccess-dds-ny.un.org/doc/RESOLUTION/GEN/NR0/348/90/IMG/NR034890.pdf?OpenElement.
17. S.C. Resolution 1189, *U.N. Doc.* S/RES/1189(1998), adopted on 13th August, 1998. Retrieved January 05, 2012 from http://www.un.org/ga/search/view_doc.asp?symbol=S/RES/1189%281998%29.
18. *The Nicaragua case,* (*Nicaragua* v. *United States of America*), International Court of Justice (ICJ), 27th June 1986. Retrieved January 06, 2012 from www.refworld.org/docid/4023a 44d2.html.
19. Second Administrative Reforms Commission, Government of India. (June 2008). *Combating Terrorism: Protecting by Righteousness*, (Eighth Report, Chapter 4). pp. 4-5. Retrieved December 02, 2011 from http://arc.gov.in/8threport/ARC_8th Report_Ch4.pdf.
20. *Ibid.*
21. Centers for Disease Control and Prevention, Bio-terrorism, CDC Emergency Risk Communication Branch (ERCB), Division of Emergency Operations (DEO), National Center for Emerging and Zoonotic Infectious Diseases (NCEZID), Atlanta, USA. Retrieved January 05, 2012 from http://www.bt.cdc.gov/bioterrorism/overview.asp.
22. *Nath, Ravinder* A. (2004). Bio-Terrorism: A Threat to National Security. In A. Subramanyam Raju (Ed.) *Terrorism in South Asia: Views from India*, (pp. 145–154). New Delhi: India Research Press.
23. *Ibid.*
24. Barnett Daniel J., and Parker Cindy L. (October, 2006). Understanding Radiologic and Nuclear Terrorism as Public

Health Threats: Preparedness and Response Perspectives, *The Journal of Nuclear Medicine, 47(10)*. Reston, USA. pp. 1653-1661.

25. Retrieved January, 05, 2012 from http://www.un.org/en/sc/ctc/docs/conventions/Conv13.pdf.
26. *Ibid.*
27. Barnett Daniel J., and Parker Cindy L. (October, 2006). Understanding Radiologic and Nuclear Terrorism as Public Health Threats: Preparedness and Response Perspectives, *The Journal of Nuclear Medicine, 47(10)*. Reston, USA. pp. 1653-1661.
28. *Ibid.*
29. *Ibid.*
30. Second Administrative Reforms Commission, Government of India. (June 2008). *Combating Terrorism: Protecting by Righteousness*, (Eighth Report, Chapter 4). pp. 6-7. Retrieved December 02, 2011 from http://arc.gov.in/8threport/ARC_8th Report_Ch.4.pdf.
31. *Ibid.*, pp. 6-7.
32. Collin, B. (March 1997). The Future of Cyberterrorism, *Crime and Justice International*, Brisbane, pp. 15-18.
33. Pollitt, M.M. (2003) "*Cyberterrorism - Fact or Fancy?*" FBI Laboratory. Retrieved January, 07, 2012 from http://www.cs.georgetown.edu/~denning/infosec/pollitt.html.
34. Garrison, L and Grand, M. "*Cyberterrorism: An evolving concept*," NIPC Highlights, 2001, Retrieved January, 07, 2012 from http://www.nipc.gov/publi-cations/highlights/2001/highlight-01-06.htm.
35. Steve Saint-Claire, *Overview and Analysis on Cyber Terrorism,* School of Doctoral Studies (European Union) Journal. Annual Open Access Publication of the School of Doctoral Studies of the European Union, Brussels, Belgium; Number 3, Year 2011, pp. 85-98. Retrieved January, 05, 2012 from http://www.iiuedu.eu/press/journals/sds/SDS_2011/SDS_2011.pdf.
36. *Ibid.*

4

DEFINITIONS OF TERRORISM

Terrorism is very common phenomenon of the world. It is very easy to recognise but very hard to define. It is hard to believe that a word like 'terrorism' which is used so frequently nowadays in different context does not have any universally accepted definition. There is no official or universal definition of terrorism agreed on all over the world. Despite decades of academic literature on the subject of terrorism no commonly accepted definition has been found. Terrorism is not a domestic or regional problem any longer. Actually, terrorism is an ever-changing issue. What is called terrorism one year may be called something else next year. Terrorists find new targets and new means to carry out attacks. This problem is to be tackle at its roots. Though it is not at all an easy task to define terrorism, but we have to overcome this problem. Actually any research on terrorism cannot be completed without defining the term terrorism. If anybody does not know what terrorism is, then no one can recognise what acts, what organisations, and what persons are terrorist. One can say by objecting that terrorism cannot be known, understood, or studied but it can be fought and eradicated. Even if this argument is taken, one nonetheless has to admit that a minimal knowledge of terrorism is necessary to fight it. How could we protect ourselves from terrorism and strike back against it if we are unable to identify it? An adequate definition of terrorism is the need of the hour to face international terrorism, which spreads across the world. Though, till today most attempts have failed to reach a unified definition for the term terrorism on both international and regional levels. There are number of international conventions which are related to terrorism. There are various definitions of terrorism both in national and international levels and every definition though it appears correct in its own perspective, lacks some important aspects of terrorism. Thus on the one hand, without a definition, it is impossible to formulate or enforce international agreements against terrorism. It is something like catching the air. Now, it seems to be very clear that the search for an adequate definition is merely like looking for a black cat in a dark room. In my opinion, instead of raising a 'what' question in this respect we should raise a question 'when to settle the issue' – when is a movement called terrorism? Instead of 'what is terrorism'?

On 18th December, 1972, the UN General Assembly, on the recommendation of the sixth committee decided to establish an Ad hoc committee on terrorism.[1] The objectives of the Committee were to provide a definition of the term international terrorism, to study the underlying causes of terrorism and to agree on recommendations for an international document aimed at the prevention of terrorism.[2] The Committee debated intensely whether the concept of terrorism should, and could, be defined. There were two conflicting views. On the one side, a definition of the term 'terrorism' was considered to be possible on the basis of the agreement. On the other side were those who responded that agreement upon definition was doomed to failure, and that it was better to proceed pragmatically with building up agreed norms that were relevant to different aspects of the overall problems. The Committee agonised over the conflicting positions, and when it reported to the General Assembly in 1979, the Committee avoided taking any attempt at definition. It was impossible to reach a final consensus concerning a generally acceptable, comprehensive definition of international terrorism together with the conclusion of an appropriate universal comprehensive convention.

Problems for Defining the Terrorism

A precise definition of terrorism has not been possible because there are several national and even local variables. Such factors as the nature and extent of motivation on the part of those who indulge in terrorist activities, their social and even physical environments, tools available to the terrorists, and also the state of crime, violence and atrocities a society is used to absorb, all these differ from one country to another. All these are relevant in order to arrive at a definition of terrorism.

There are various reasons for not defining the term terrorism by the international community. The problems for defining the term terrorism may be the followings :

(i) The first reason deals with sovereignty. Nations reserve the right to define legal bounds of activities and policies within their own borders. Therefore each state reserves the right to determine, politically and legally what terrorism is. No nation wants to be constrained by a definition which would inhibit its own foreign and domestic policy.

(ii) Some United Nations member nations use terrorism for their own purposes and are not about to agree to any limitation on their actions. Until all members of the United Nations agree to stop harbouring, training and sponsoring terrorists, the United Nations will not be the appropriate forum to develop a co-ordinated definition or policy to prevent and respond to terrorism.

(iii) It is necessary to distinguish between three different conceptions of terrorism – terrorism as a crime in itself, terrorism as a method to perpetrate other crimes, and terrorism as an act of war. When terrorism is conceived of as a crime, its elements and defences can be identified and analysed. When terrorism is conceived of as a method to perpetrate other crimes, terrorism will sometimes overlap with other crimes like crimes against humanity, genocide, war crimes, rape, etc. When terrorism is conceived of as an act of war, the laws of war will cover the legal responses to terrorism.

(iv) The mass media have contributed to the confusion about the meaning of terrorism by often using the term terrorism in a rather superficial manner, by shifting the political discourse from 'issues' to 'episodes', transforming politics into entertainment and moving from opinion making to stimulation through pictures.

(v) Terrorism cannot be defined because it is impossible to isolate the traits that belong to this type of violence. Terrorism is only the activity of the enemy, whoever the enemy may be and whatever his activity may be. One cannot define terrorism independently of the point of view one adopts. Everyone, when defining terrorism, actually describes the acts of violence carried out by his own enemy so that the indefinite extension of the concept overwhelms and destroys its comprehension.

(vi) Another problem in defining terrorism is that different types of group exist. Some groups, such as the Liberation Tigers of Tamil Eelam (LTTE) are separatist groups with their own independent agenda (the LTTE wants its own independent Tamil state in Sri Lanka); they generally confine their attacks to domestic political and military targets, economic infrastructure, and civilians. For these groups, it is essential for the any country to develop a clear definition and policy regarding their actions, because such groups are a direct threat not only to citizens of many countries, but to the vital international security interests of many nations.

(vii) The notion of terrorism is quite complicated and terrorist acts may be part of insurgency and subversion.

(viii) Terrorism is a phenomenon which appears under different guises and according to some nation it is not possible to agree on a definition of terrorism unless the causes of terrorism are considered.

Reasons for Defining Terrorism

In the absence of a definition, there is a free and open tendency for the persons using the term, whether states, organised groups or scholars; to define it as suits their purposes at the moment to describe different forms of conduct.[3] Hence, it is important to define the word 'terrorism' for the following reasons:

(i) *Legislation and punishment* – The laws and regulations relating to security forces are enacted for the purpose of combating terrorism. A definition of terrorism is necessary when legislating laws designed to ban terrorism and assistance to terrorism, as well as when setting minimum sentences for terrorists or confiscating their financial resources and supplies. If there is no accepted definition, these legislations have no value. Legislation and punishment must distinguish terrorism from ordinary crime, even when they might actually be identical in practice. A workable or working definition would be required with a view to have special laws for tackling terrorism within the country and to get terrorists extradited from abroad.[4] It is somewhat surprising that despite terrorism being recognised as a global phenomenon, attempts in the past for arriving at an internationally accepted definition of terrorism have proved futile. According to the said report, this ambivalence is primarily due to two reasons *firstly*, a 'terrorist' in one country may be viewed as a 'freedom fighter' in another; *secondly*, it is known that some states resort to or encourage various kinds of criminal acts, secretly, through their own agencies or hired agents to subvert or to otherwise destabilise another lawfully established government or in extreme cases get important political or governmental personalities of another State assassinated.[5] Whenever any international community or any individual state is adopting any counter-terrorism law and policy, it depends on the definition of terrorism. This basic question is of the utmost importance in determining who a state or international body will consider a terrorist and, therefore, who will be subject to the stricter laws and harsher penalties that are associated with the definition of terrorism.

(ii) *International co-operation* – An internationally accepted definition of terrorism is required to strengthen co-operation between countries in the struggle against terrorism, and to ensure its effectiveness. Terrorism is no longer a local problem of specific countries but an issue involving a number of international aspects. Without a definition of terrorism, it is impossible to formulate or enforce international agreements against terrorism. One of the conspicuous examples of the need to define terrorism concerns the extradition of terrorists. Although many countries have signed bilateral and multi-lateral agreements concerning a variety of crimes but extradition for political offences is often explicitly excluded. Generally as the background of terrorism is always political, this loophole allows many countries to shirk their obligation to extradite individuals wanted for terrorist activities.

(iii) *States sponsoring terrorism* – Nowadays, terrorism is increasingly dependent on the support of nations. States sponsoring terrorism use terrorist organisations as a means to their own ends, while these organisations depend on the assistance they receive from such countries at the eco-military, and operational levels. Some organisations are so closely dependent on the assistance of states that they become 'puppets' functioning at the initiative, direction, and with the complete support of these states. It is impossible to contend effectively with terrorism without severing the close tie between the terrorist organisations and the sponsoring states. This tie, however, cannot be severed without agreeing on a broad definition of terrorism, and thus of the states that sponsor it and of the steps to be taken against them.

(iv) *Universally accepted definition* – In absence of comprehensive and universally accepted definition of terrorism, it is an obstacle to construct a unified global stance against terrorism and, also to know the meaning, implementation, and effect of United Nations resolutions and international treaties involving counter-terrorism issues. The absence of a universal definition of terrorism will obstruct counter-terrorism operations and limits the effectiveness of both international and domestic law-making efforts to counter-terrorist activity while maintaining the rule of law and fulfilling human rights obligations.

(v) *Separation from other violent actions* – A definition that separates terrorism out from other forms of violence will enable the initiation of an international campaign designed to undermine the legitimacy of terrorist organisations, curtail support for them, and galvanise a united international front against them. In order to undermine the legitimacy of terrorist activity, it should be distinguished from guerrilla activity, war, crimes, insurgency etc.

(vi) *Offensive action* – To ensure international support for States struggling against terrorism, and perhaps even for a joint offensive, an internationally accepted definition of terrorism is required that will distinguish freedom fighting from terrorist activity. The State struggling against terrorism must retain the initiative. At the same time, attempts must be made to limit, as for as possible, the operative capacity of the terrorist organisation. To attain these aims, a continued offensive must be conducted against terrorist organisations.

Terrorism and Freedom Fighter

Terrorist organisations often put up a shield of nomenclatures by equating their acts with freedom fighter. It is frequently described by very common and popular phrase – "one man's terrorist is another man's freedom fighter." A true 'freedom fighter' is usually a peaceful, non-violent dissident, who is outspoken on matters of political reform and often jailed for their beliefs. Examples of 'freedom fighter' include Mahatma Gandhi, Subhas Chandra Bose, Nelson Mandela, Martin Luther King Jr., Aung San San Suu Kyi etc. A terrorist is a person, who indulges in criminal acts regardless of territorial limitations, innocent bystanders and neutral countries for his political and ideological motives. He does not recognise legal order and public support. He takes resort to acts inspiring terror without exhausting legitimate remedies at his disposal for getting redressal for his grievances. A freedom fighter, on the other hand, does not essential target innocent persons. His acts represent common conscience of the people. Freedom fighter is a person, who has been a victim of alien, illegal or repressive regime for quite some time without any access to effective legitimate remedies for his sufferings; therefore he exercises his right of self-determination against such a regime. The acts of freedom fighter might be compatible with the UN Charter, the *Declaration on Friendly Relation, and International Humanitarian Law*.[6] A freedom fighter fights against the regime or government which made him a victim for quite some time, and which is responsible for his sufferings. He does not have any access to effective legitimate remedies for his sufferings; therefore he exercises his right to self-determination. The idea that one person's terrorist is another's freedom fighter cannot be sanctioned. Freedom fighters or revolutionaries do not blow up buses containing non-combatants; terrorist murderers do. Freedom fighters do not set out to capture and slaughter school children' terrorist murderers do. Freedom fighters do not assassinate innocent businessman, or hijack and hold hostage innocent men, women and children; terrorist murderers do. The treasured word 'freedom' cannot be associated with acts of terrorists.

Another thing, in truth, individuals have various identities – a man may be father and murderer, husband and rapist. Even we also share a multiplicity of different identities – such as, we may be at particular times, workers, shoppers, hosts or guests. On this reasoning, a man may be both terrorist and freedom fighter. But the latter identity rests on his motives – what he is fighting for and the former relates to the methods he adopts in this fight – the targetting, specially, of civilians, to achieve his ends. Terrorism, thus conceived, can be adopted for one among many motives – to fight for freedom, for particular environmental policies, for a ban on abortions, for animal rights, among others – and remains terrorism as long as the method or means utilised involve the intentional targetting of civilians. If, however, terrorism is defined strictly in terms of attacks non-military targets various attacks on military installations and soldier's residence would easily escape from the ambit of the definition.

Most civilised nations by way of framing laws identified the modes of conduct that are criminal, such as homicide, kidnapping, threats to life, the willful destruction of property. But such laws may not be applicable in case of war. In war there are rules which outlaw the use of certain weapons and tactics. The rules of war grant civilian non-combatants immunity from deliberate attack. They prohibit taking civilian hostages and actions against those held captive. The rules of war recognise no neutral territory, non-combatants, and no bystanders. They often seize, threaten and murder hostages. So, it can be easily said that one man's terrorist is everyone's terrorist. A man, on this reasoning, may be both terrorist and freedom fighter.

Various Definitions of Terrorism

At present there exists plethora of definitions of terrorism both at the national and international levels. The United Nations and other International Organisations have tried to hold ad hoc conventions dealing with terrorism. Since 1963, many conventions have been held by the International Organisations related to prevention and suppression of terrorism. But there does not exist a single definition of terrorism acceptable to even majority of the international community. All definitions seek to address the various aspects of terrorism from motive, to finance to modus etc. Some of the definitions in national, international and regional levels are mentioned below.

(i) League of Nation's Convention for the Prevention and Punishment of Terrorism, 1937

After the First World War terrorist activities gradually increased, accordingly in the late 1920 and early 1930 first international attempt was made to define terrorism. Terrorism was more systematically considered in a series of International Conferences for the Unification of Criminal Law between 1930 and 1935. Terrorism was discussed at the 3rd (Brussels 1930), 4th (Paris 1931), 5th (Madrid 1933) and 6th (Copenhagen 1935) International Conferences for the Unification of Criminal Law.[7] The term 'terrorism' was used for the first time in an international penal instrument at the third (Brussels) international conference for the unification of penal law in the year 1930.[8] At the Fourth Conference in Paris in 1931, two rapporteurs proposed different definitions, although each shared the core element of imposing a political or social doctrine through criminal violence.[9] At the Fifth Conference in Madrid in 1934, terrorism and crimes creating a common danger were considered separately and the discussion focussed on terrorism. In 1935, the Sixth Conference at Copenhagen adopted model national legislation for the repression of terrorism.[10]

The Sixth Conference adopted a text that defined terrorism in Article 1, which is as follows[11] :

> "International acts directed against the life, physical integrity, health or freedom of a head of state or his spouse, or any person holding the prerogatives of a head of state, as well as crown princes, members of governments, people enjoying diplomatic immunity, and members of the constitutional, legislative or judicial bodies [if the perpetrator creates] a common danger, or a state of terror that might incite a change or raise an obstacle to the functioning of public bodies or a disturbance to international relations."

The most significant early modern attempt to define terrorism as an international crime was undertaken by the League of Nations between 1934 and 1937. In October 1934, King Alexander I of Yugoslavia was assassinated by Croatian separatists while on a State visit to France[12]; the French Foreign Minister, Louis Barthou, and two by-standers were also killed. The suspects fled to Italy and France requested their extradition under a treaty of 1870, which excluded political crimes from extradition. The Court of Appeal of Turin refused to surrender the accused on the ground that the offences were politically motivated and thus non-extraditable.[13] France proposed that 'international measures' should be taken to address the problem.

The League had faced a similar international crisis in 1923, when General Tellini of Italy was assassinated while delimiting the frontier between Albania and Greece, resulting in Italy's bombardment and occupation of Corfu.[14] In July 1934, Austrian Chancellor Dollfuss was assassinated by ten Austrian Nazis, which was still fresh.[15] Seasoned diplomats had not forgotten the assassination of Archduke Franz Ferdinand in Sarajevo in 1914 and its catastrophic consequences for global peace.[16]

Later in the year 1935, the League of Nations established an expert committee, namely Committee for the International Repression of Terrorism (CIRT), to draft a preliminary international convention 'to assure the repression of conspiracies or crimes committed with a political and terrorist purpose. The terms 'terrorist activity' and 'political and terrorist purpose' were not defined. The CIRT comprised eleven States (Belgium, Chile, France, Hungary, Italy, Poland, Romania, Spain, Switzerland, U.K., and USSR) and met in three sessions between April 1935 and April 1937. The convention was drafted in a number of phases between 1935 and 1937. An international diplomatic conference met in November 1937 to draft and adopt a convention based on the final draft submitted by CIRT. The Final Act of the diplomatic conference adopted two international conventions—the first defining international terrorist offences, and the second creating an international criminal court to punish the offences in the first treaty. The League of Nations faced political pressure, which resulted for drafting of *Convention for the Prevention and Punishment of Terrorism (1937 Terrorism Convention)*.[17] International efforts to curb terrorists acts first found expression in this League of Nation's *Convention for the Prevention and Punishment of Terrorism (1937 Terrorism Convention)*.[18] After the establishment of League of Nation, it is for the first time took the initiative to outlaw the menace of terrorism, which was signed by 24 nations but ratified ultimately only by one nation, India. It was signed on 16th November, 1937 though it never entered into force. This 1937 Terrorism Convention required States to criminalise terrorist offences and encouraged States to exclude the offences from the political offence exception to extradition. The Convention was only ratified by one (colonial) State - India.

This Convention defined 'acts of terrorism' as "criminal acts directed against a State and intended or calculated to create a state of terror in the minds of particular persons or a group of persons or the general public."[19] According to this Convention 'terrorist acts' means as follows[20]

"1. Any willful act causing death or grievous bodily harm or loss of liberty to:
   (a) Heads of State, persons exercising the prerogatives of the head of the State, their hereditary or designated successors;
   (b) The wives or husbands or the above-mentioned persons;
   (c) Persons charged with public functions or holding public positions when the act is directed against them in their public capacity.
2. Willful destruction of, or damage to, public property or property devoted to a public purpose belonging to or subject to the authority of another High Contracting Party.
3. Any willful act calculated to endanger the lives of members of the public.
4. Any attempt to commit an offence falling within the foregoing provisions of the present article.
5. The manufacture, obtaining, possession, or supplying of arms, ammunition, explosives or harmful substances with the view to the commission in any country whatsoever of an offence falling within the present article."

The League of Nations itself soon dissolved as a result of the World War- II, and subsequent efforts to define terrorism were unsuccessful. The World War II, diverted attention from the Convention and with the demise of the League of Nations, interest in the Convention never revived. This definition is also inadequate for several reasons. First, this definition makes no reference to the illegality of politically motivated acts of violence, such as murder and kidnapping of civilians. Another important problem with this definition is that it defines terrorism in terms of victim (non-combatants) instead of the perpetrators and their motives. But one cannot over estimate its importance as the first comprehensive and multi-lateral anti-terrorist convention. It is interesting that till today the definition given in this convention is taken as a core definition and the main characteristics of the definition has remained unchanged even after more than seventy years.

(ii) Many Definitions of Terrorism by Different Scholars and Recognised Experts

Alex Peter Schmid is an internationally renowned Dutch scholar in Terrorism Studies and also former Officer-in-Charge of the Terrorism Prevention Branch of the United Nations and Director of its Centre for the Study of Terrorism and Political Violence (CSTPV). In their book, Schmid and Youngman cited 109 different definitions of terrorism depending upon their study till 1988 and the number would be far higher today. They defined the terrorism as follows:[21]

> "Terrorism is an anxiety-inspiring method of repeated violent action, employed by (semi-) clandestine individual, group or state actors, for idiosyncratic, criminal or political reasons, whereby – in contrast to assassination - the direct targets of violence are not the main targets. The immediate human victims of violence are generally chosen randomly (targets of opportunity) or selectively (representative or symbolic targets) from a target population, and serve as message generators. Threat and violence-based communication processes between terrorist (organisation), (imperiled) victims, and main targets are used to manipulate the main target (audience(s)), turning it into a target of terror, a target of demands, or a target of attention, depending on whether intimidation, coercion, or propaganda is primarily sought."

M. Cherif Bassiouni, who is one of the World's leading experts in the field of International Criminal Law, has also proposed a definition of terrorism.[22]

> "Ideologically-motivated strategy of internationally prescribed violence designed to inspire terror with in a particular segment of a given society in order to achieve a power outcome or to propagandise a claim or grievance irrespective of whether its perpetrators are acting for and on behalf of themselves or on behalf of a state."

Yonah Alexander has defined terrorism as[23] –

> "The use of violence against random civilian targets in order to intimidate or to create generalised pervasive fear for the purpose of achieving political goals."

Bruce Hoffman has defined terrorism as follows[24] –

> "Terrorism is ineluctably political in aims and motives, violence or, equally important, threatens violence, designed to have far-reaching psychological repercussions beyond the immediate victim or target, conducted by an organisation with an identifiable chain of command or conspiratorial cell structure (whose members wear no uniform or identifying insignia), and perpetrated by a sub-national group or non-state entity."

Rosalyn Higgins, who was the Judge at International Court of Justice, defined terrorism as[25] –

> "Terrorism is a term without any legal significance. It is merely a convenient way of alluding to activities, whether of States or individuals widely disapproves of and in which wither the methods used are unlawful, or the targets protected or both."

Louise Richardson commented on terrorism as follows[26] –

> "The only universally accepted attribute of them 'terrorism' is that it pejorative. Terrorism is something that bad guys do."

Instead of defining what terrorism is, some authors, e.g., Thomas H. Mitchell, propose a negative definition[27] –

"A definition of terrorism must clearly establish what terrorism is not."

(iii) Definitions of Terrorism in Different Dictionaries and Encyclopaedias

In Encyclopaedia Britannica, terrorism is defined as follows[28] –

> "The systematic use of violence to create a general climate of fear in a population and thereby to bring about a particular political objective. Terrorism has been practised by political organisations with both rightist and leftist objectives, by nationalistic and religious groups, by revolutionaries, and even by state institutions such as armies, intelligence services, and police."

According to Black's Law Dictionary terrorism means[29] –

> "The use or threat of violence to intimidate or cause apprehension and panic, especially, as a means of affecting political conduct."

Chambers 21st Century Dictionary, terrorism is defined as[30] –

> "The systematic and organised use of violence and intimidation to force a government or community etc., to act in a certain way or accept certain demands."

In Oxford Advanced Learner's Dictionary, terrorism is mentioned as[31]

> "The use of violent action in order to achieve political aims or to force a government to act."

(iv) *International Law Commission on Terrorism*

The International Law Commission has defined the term terrorism to include[32] –

(1) Any act causing death or grievous bodily harm or loss of liberty to head of state, persons exercising the prerogative of the Head of State, their hereditary or designated successors, the spouse of such persons, or person charged with public functions or holding public opinions when the act is directed against them in their public capacity;

(2) Acts calculated to destroy or damage public property or property devoted to public purpose;

(3) Any act likely to imperil human lives through the creation of a public danger, in particular, the seizure of Aircraft, the taking of hostages and any form of violence directed against persons, who enjoy international protection or diplomatic immunity;

(4) The manufacture, obtaining possession or supplying of arms, ammunitions, explosives or harmful substances with a view to the commission of terrorist act."

(v) *Definition of Terrorism in Different Countries United Kingdom*

The United Kingdom was one of the first states to specifically criminalise terrorism. According to Terrorism Act, 2000 of United Kingdom defines terrorism as follows:[33]

(1) In this Act, "terrorism" means the use or threat of action where –

- (a) the action falls within sub-section (2),
- (b) the use or threat is designed to influence the government or an international governmental organisation or to intimidate the public or a section of the public, and
- (c) the use or threat is made for the purpose of advancing a political, religious or ideological cause.

(2) Action falls within this sub-section if it—

- (a) involves serious violence against a person,
- (b) involves serious damage to property,
- (c) endangers a person's life, other than that of the person committing the action,
- (d) creates a serious risk to the health or safety of the public or a section of the public, or
- (e) is designed seriously to interfere with or seriously to disrupt an electronic system.

(3) The use or threat of action falling within sub-section (2) which involves the use of firearms or explosives is terrorism

whether or not sub-section (1)(b) is satisfied.

(4) In this section –

(a) "action" includes action outside the United Kingdom,

(b) a reference to any person or to property is a reference to any person, or to property, wherever situated,

(c) a reference to the public includes a reference to the public of a country other than the United Kingdom, and "the government" means the government of the United Kingdom, of a Part of the United Kingdom or of a country other than the United Kingdom."

After passing the Terrorism Act, 2006, definition of terrorism as given in the Terrorism Act, 2000 was slightly amended. According to the Section 34 of the new Act of 2006,[34] after 'government' in Section 1(1)(b) of the previous Act, 2000 'or an international government organisation' has been added.

Canada

In Canada, the Canadian Criminal Code, 2002, defines 'terrorist activity' as follows[35] –

"terrorist activity" means

(a) an act or omission that is committed in or outside Canada and that, if committed in Canada, is one of the following offences:

(i) the offences referred to in sub-section 7(2) that implement the *Convention for the Suppression of Unlawful Seizure of Aircraft*, signed at The Hague on December 16, 1970.

(ii) the offences referred to in sub-section 7(2) that implement the *Convention for the Suppression of Unlawful Acts against the Safety of Civil Aviation*, signed at Montreal on September 23, 1971.

(iii) the offences referred to in sub-section 7(3) that implement the *Convention on the Prevention and Punishment of Crimes against Internationally Protected Persons, including Diplomatic Agents*, adopted by the General Assembly of the United Nations on December 14, 1973.,

(iv) the offences referred to in sub-section 7(3.1) that implement the *International Convention against the Taking of Hostages*, adopted by the General Assembly of the United Nations on December 17, 1979.

(v) the offences referred to in sub-section 7(3.4) or (3.6) that implement the *Convention on the Physical Protection of Nuclear Material*, done at Vienna and New York on March 3, 1980.

(vi) the offences referred to in sub-section 7(2) that implement the *Protocol for the Suppression of Unlawful Acts of Violence at Airports Serving International Civil Aviation*, supplementary to the *Convention for the Suppression of Unlawful Acts against the Safety of Civil Aviation*, signed at Montreal on February 24, 1988.

(vii) the offences referred to in sub-section 7(2.1) that implement the *Convention for the Suppression of Unlawful Acts against the Safety of Maritime Navigation*, done at Rome on March 10, 1988.

(viii) the offences referred to in sub-section 7(2.1) or (2.2) that implement the *Protocol for the Suppression of Unlawful Acts against the Safety of Fixed Platforms Located on the Continental Shelf*, done at Rome on March 10, 1988.

(ix) the offences referred to in sub-section 7(3.72) that implement the *International Convention for the Suppression of Terrorist Bombings*, adopted by the General Assembly of the United Nations on December 15, 1997,

(x) the offences referred to in sub-section 7(3.73) that implement the *International Convention for the Suppression of the Financing of Terrorism*, adopted by the General Assembly of the United Nations on December 9, 1999,

(a) an act or omission, in or outside Canada,

(i) that is committed,

(A) in whole or in part for a political, religious or ideological purpose, objective or cause,

(B) in whole or in part with the intention of intimidating the public, or a segment of the public, with regard to its security, including its economic security, or compelling a person, a government or a domestic or an international organisation to do or to refrain from doing any act, whether the public or the person, government or organisation is inside or outside Canada,

(ii) that intentionally,

(A) causes death or serious bodily harm to a person by the use of violence,

(B) endangers a person's life,

(C) causes a serious risk to the health or safety of the public or any segment of the public,

(D) causes substantial property damage, whether to public or private property, if causing such damage is likely to result in the conduct or harm referred to in any of clauses (A) to (C),

(E) causes serious interference with or serious disruption of an essential service, facility or system, whether public or private, other than as a result of advocacy, protest, dissent or stoppage of work that is not intended to result in the conduct or harm referred to in any of clauses (A) to (C), and includes a conspiracy, attempt or threat to commit any such act or omission, or being an accessory after the fact or counselling in relation to any such act or omission, but, for greater certainty, does not include an act or omission that is committed during an armed conflict and that, at the time and in the place of its commission, is in accordance with customary international law or conventional international law applicable to the conflict, or the activities undertaken by military forces of a state in the exercise of their official duties, to the extent that those activities are governed by other rules of international law."

Australia

In Australia, the *Criminal Code Amendment (Terrorism) Act, 2003,* defines 'terrorist act' as follows[36] –

(1) "................terrorist act means an action or threat of action where:

(a) the action falls within sub-section (2) and does not fall within sub-section (3);

(b) the action is done or the threat is made with the intention of advancing a political, religious or ideological cause;

(c) the action is done or the threat is made with the intention of:

(i) coercing, or influencing by intimidation, the government of the Commonwealth or a State, Territory or foreign country, or of part of a State, Territory or foreign country;

(ii) Intimidating the public or a section of the public.

(2) Action falls within this sub-section if it:

(a) causes serious harm that is physical harm to a person; or

(b) causes serious damage to property;

(c) causes a person's death;

(d) endangers a person's life, other than the life of the person taking the action;

(e) creates a serious risk to the health or safety of the public or a section of the public;

(f) seriously interferes with, seriously disrupts, or destroys, an electronic system including, but not limited to:

(i) an information system;

(ii) a telecommunications system;

(iii) a financial system;

(iv) a system used for the delivery of essential government services;

(v) a system used for, or by, an essential public utility;

(vi) a system used for, or by, a transport system.

(3) Action falls within this sub-section if it:

(a) is advocacy, protest, dissent or industrial action;

(b) is not intended:

(i) to cause serious harm that is physical harm to a person;

(ii) to cause a person's death;

(iii) to endanger the life of a person, other than the person taking the action;

(iv) to create a serious risk to the health or safety of the public or a section of the public."

New Zealand

In New Zealand, Terrorism Suppression Act, 2002, defines 'terrorist act' as follows[37]–

(1) An act is a terrorist act for the purposes of this Act if -

(a) the act falls within sub-section (2);

(b) the act is an act against a specified terrorism convention (as defined in section 4(1) ;

(c) the act is a terrorist act in armed conflict (as defined in section 4(1)).

(2) An act falls within this sub-section if it is intended to cause, in any one or more countries, one or more of the outcomes specified in sub-section (3) and is carried out for the purpose of advancing an ideological, political, or religious cause, and with the following intention:

(a) to induce terror in a civilian population;

(b) to unduly compel or to force a government or an international organisation to do or abstain from doing any act.

(3) The outcomes referred to in sub-section (2) are:

(a) the death of, or other serious bodily injury to, one or more persons (other than a person carrying out the act):

(b) a serious risk to the health or safety of a population:

(c) destruction of, or serious damage to, property of great value or importance, or major economic loss, or major environmental damage, if likely to result in one or more outcomes specified in paragraphs (a), (b), and (d):

(d) serious interference with, or serious disruption to, an infrastructure facility, if likely to endanger human life:

(e) introduction or release of a disease-bearing organism, if likely to devastate the national economy of a country.

(4) However, an act does not fall within sub-section (2), if it occurs in a situation of armed conflict and is, at the time and in the place that it occurs, in accordance with rules of international law applicable to the conflict.

(5) To avoid doubt, the fact that a person engages in any protest, advocacy, or dissent, or engages in any strike, lock-out, or other industrial action, is not, by itself, a sufficient basis for inferring that the person -

(a) is carrying out an act for a purpose, or with an intention, specified in sub-section (2);

(b) intends to cause an outcome specified in sub-section (3).

France

In the French Penal Code, the term 'acts of terrorism' has mentioned in the following manner[38]–

"The following offences constitute acts of terrorism where they are committed intentionally in connection with an individual or collective undertaking the purpose of which is seriously to disturb public order through intimidation or terror:

1. willful attacks on life, willful attacks on the physical integrity of persons, abduction and unlawful detention and also as the hijacking of planes, vessels or any other means of transport, defined by Book II of the present Code;
2. theft, extortion, destruction, defacement and damage, and also computer offences, as defined under Book III of the present Code;
3. offences committed by combat organisations and disbanded movements as defined under Articles 431-13 to 431-17, and the offences set out under Articles 434-6, 441-2 to 441-5;
4. the production or keeping of machines, dangerous or explosive devices, set out under Article 3 of the Act of 19 June, 1871, which repealed the Decree of 4th September, 1870, on the production of military grade weapons;

- the production, sale, import or export of explosive substances as defined by Article 6 of the Act no. 70-575 of 3rd July, 1970, amending the regulations governing explosive powders and substances;
- the purchase, keeping, transport or unlawful carrying of explosive substances or of devices made with such explosive substances, as defined by Article 38 of the Ordinance of 18

April, 1939 defining the regulations governing military equipment, weapons and ammunition;

- the detention, carrying, and transport of weapons and ammunition falling under the first and fourth categories defined by Articles 4, 28, 31 and 32 of the aforementioned Ordinance;
- the offences defined by Articles 1 and 4 of the Act No. 72-467 of 9th June, 1972, forbidding the designing, production, keeping, stocking, purchase or sale of biological or toxin-based weapons;
- the offences referred to under Articles 58 to 63 of the Act No. 98-467 of 17th June, 1998 on the application of the Convention of the 13 January, 1993 on the prohibition of developing, producing, stocking and use of chemical weapons and on their destruction;

5. receiving the product of one of the offences set out in paragraphs 1 to 4 above;
6. the money laundering offences set out in Chapter IV of title II of Book III of the present Code;
7. the insider trading offences set out in article L.465-1 of the Financial and Monetary Code."

United States

United States Department of Defence defines terrorism as follows[39]–

> "The unlawful use of violence or threat of violence to instill fear and coerce governments or societies. Terrorism is often motivated by religious, political, or other ideological beliefs and committed in the pursuit of goals that are usually political."

United States Law Code which governs the entire United States defines terrorism as[40] –

"Premeditated, politically motivated violence perpetrated against non-combatant targets by sub-national groups or clandestine agents, usually intended to influence an audience."

Title 18 (regarding *Crimes and Criminal Procedure*), Chapter 113-B of the US Code defines 'international terrorism' and 'domestic terrorism.' According to sub-section (1) of the said Chapter international terrorism means[41]–

"Activities that –

(A) involve violent acts or acts dangerous to human life that are a violation of the criminal laws of the United States or of any State, or that would be a criminal violation, if committed within the jurisdiction of the United States or of any State;

(B) appear to be intended –

(i) to intimidate or coerce a civilian population;

(ii) to influence the policy of a government by intimidation or coercion;

(iii) to affect the conduct of a government by mass destruction, assassination, or kidnapping;

(C) occur primarily outside the territorial jurisdiction of the United States, or transcend national boundaries in terms of the means by which they are accomplished, the persons they appear intended to intimidate or coerce, or the locale in which their perpetrators operate or seek asylum."

According to sub-section (5) of the said Chapter, international terrorism means[120] –

"Activities that –

(A) involve acts dangerous to human life that are a violation of the criminal laws of the United States or of any State;

(B) appear to be intended –

(i) to intimidate or coerce a civilian population;

(ii) to influence the policy of a government by intimidation or coercion;

(iii) to affect the conduct of a government by mass destruction, assassination, or kidnapping; and

(C) occur primarily within the territorial jurisdiction of the United States."

Following September 11, the United States passed Uniting and Strengthening America by providing Appropriate Tools Required to

Intercept and Obstruct Terrorism (Usa Patriot) Act, 2001, which amended the said Section 2331, Title 18 of the US Code as follows[42]–

"(1) the term 'international terrorism' means activities that –

(A) involve violent acts or acts dangerous to human life that are a violation of the criminal laws of the United States or of any State, or that would be a criminal violation if committed within the jurisdiction of the United States or of any State;

(B) appear to be intended –

(i) to intimidate or coerce a civilian population;

(ii) to influence the policy of a government by intimidation or coercion;

(iii) to affect the conduct of a government by mass destruction, assassination, or kidnapping;

(C) occur primarily outside the territorial jurisdiction of the United States, or transcend national boundaries in terms of the means by which they are accomplished, the persons they appear intended to intimidate or coerce, or the locale in which their perpetrators operate or seek asylum;

(2) the term "national of the United States" has the meaning given such term in Section 101(a)(22) of the Immigration and Nationality Act;

(3) the term "person" means any individual or entity capable of holding a legal or beneficial interest in property;

(4) the term "act of war" means any act occurring in the course of –

(A) declared war;

(B) armed conflict, whether or not war has been declared, between two or more nations;

(C) armed conflict between military forces of any origin; and

(5) the term "domestic terrorism" means activities that -

(A) involve acts dangerous to human life that are a violation of the criminal laws of the United States or of any State;

(B) appear to be intended –

(i) to intimidate or coerce a civilian population;

(ii) to influence the policy of a government by intimidation or coercion;

(iii) to affect the conduct of a government by mass destruction, assassination, or kidnapping;

(C) occur primarily within the territorial jurisdiction of the United States.

USA PATRIOT Act, 2001 also amended Section 3077(1) of title 18, United States Code, which read as follows[43] –

"(1) 'act of terrorism' means an act of domestic or international terrorism as defined in Section 2331".

(vi) *General Assembly on Terrorism*

The General Assembly unable to agree on a definition of terrorism. But lack of agreement on a definition does not mean that the international organisations have made no attempt in combating terrorism.

In its Resolution 49/60 (A/RES/49/60), relating to Declaration on Measures to Eliminate International Terrorism the United Nations General Assembly describes terrorism as[44]–

> "Criminal acts intended or calculated to provoke a state of terror in the general public, a group of persons or particular persons for political purposes are in any circumstance unjustifiable, whatever the considerations of a political, philosophical, ideological, racial, ethnic, religious or any other nature that may be invoked to justify them."

This mandate continued to be revised and renewed on an annual basis by the General Assembly in its resolutions on the agenda item 'Measures to eliminate international terrorism'. This "definition" was cited throughout this subsequent resolutions issued up till today[45].

The then UN Secretary General, Kofi Annan, in his landmark report on United Nations reform, 'In larger freedom'[46] also proposed a definition of terrorism. The Secretary-General urged States to define terrorism as –

> "Any act intended to cause death or serious bodily harm to civilians or non-combatants, when the purpose of such an act, by its nature or context, is to intimidate a population or to compel a Government or an international organisation to do or to abstain from doing any act."

In 1996, India presented a draft of a *Comprehensive Convention on International Terrorism* (CCIT) to the Ad Hoc Committee of the UN General Assembly on International Terrorism. Article 2 of the Indian proposal defines terrorism as follows[47]–

"1. Any person commits an offence within the meaning of this Convention if that person, by any means, unlawfully and intentionally, does an act intended to cause:

(a) Death or serious bodily injury to any person;

(b) Serious damage to a State or government facility, a public transportation system, communication system or infrastructure facility with the intent to cause extensive destruction of such a place, facility or system, or where such destruction results or is likely to result in major economic loss; when the purpose of such act, by its nature or context, is to intimidate a population, or to compel a Government or an international organisation to do or abstain from doing any act.

2. Any person also commits an offence if that person attempts to commit an offence or participates as an accomplice in an offence as set forth in paragraph –

3. Any person also commits an offence if that person:

(a) Organises, directs or instigates others to commit an offence as set forth in paragraph 1 or 2;

(b) Aids, abets, facilitates or counsels the commission of such an offence;

(c) In any other way contributes to the commission of one or more offences referred to in paragraphs 1, 2 or 3 (a) by a group of persons acting with a common purpose; such contribution shall be intentional and either be made with the aim of furthering the general criminal activity or purpose of the group or be made in the knowledge of the intention of the group to commit the offence or offences concerned."

(vii) *Security Council on Terrorism*

Since the year 1980, the UN Security Council identified particular terrorist acts or methods as threats to international peace and security, such as hostage taking, hijacking and abduction; assassination; use of plastic explosives or weapons of mass destruction by non-State actors; and bombings of civilians, aircraft, embassies and UN offices. In order to define terrorism, the United Nations Security Council has established two partial measures -- first, by enacting resolutions that condemn acts of terrorism without defining the parameters of terrorism, such as Resolutions 1297, 1368 etc., secondly, by including general descriptions of acts that fall within terrorist activity without purporting to fully define terrorism, Such as Resolutions 1269, 1624, 1566 etc. The Security Council has expressed in its resolutions 1269 (1999) and 1566 (2004) that all acts of terrorism are unjustifiable regardless of their motivation.[48]

Just after the terrorist attack on 11th September, 2001, the Security Council of United Nations took a bold step to combat terrorism. The Security Council in its resolution 1373 (2001), under the powers of Chapter-VII of the UN Charter, (which makes it legally binding to member states) required member states to take specific steps in their legislation to combat the scourge of terrorism. It also decides that States shall prevent and punish financing, planning, preparation or perpetration of terrorist acts, also covering suppression of recruitment of terrorists, early warning and information sharing, movement of terrorists and trafficking of arms, explosives and dangerous materials, border controls and the obligation to follow international law when addressing refugee issues, in particular international human rights and humanitarian law.[49] While Resolution 1373 requires States to take action, it does not set out what are 'terrorist acts', the target of that action, leaving this to the States themselves. Under the Resolution 1373 (2001), a *Counter Terrorism Committee (CTC)* was established, which consists of all the 15 Members of the Security Council with the mandate to monitor the implementation of its anti-terrorism efforts. The Committee monitors the implementation of resolution 1373 (2001) by all States and tries to increase the capability of States to fight terrorism.

Resolution 1566, unanimously approved by the Security Council in October 2004, remedies the absence of a definition in Resolution 1373 to some extent. Like previous Security Council and General Assembly Resolutions, Resolution 1566 condemns terrorism in all its forms, irrespective of its motivation, and urges states to co-operate fully in the 'fight against terrorism'. Paragraph 3 of this resolution, referred terrorism as follows[50] –

> "Criminal acts, including against civilians, committed with the intent to cause death or serious bodily injury, or taking of hostages, with the purpose to provoke a state of terror in the general public or in a group of persons or particular persons, intimidate a population or compel a government or an international organisation to do or to abstain from doing any act."

(viii) *Definitions by Different United Nations Convention and Others Conventions*

Article 2 of the *International Convention for the Suppression of Terrorist Bombings, 1997* defines the offence of terrorist bombing as follows[130] -

"1. Any person commits an offence within the meaning of this Convention if that person unlawfully and intentionally delivers, places, discharges or detonates an explosive or other lethal device in, into or against a place of public use, a State or government facility, a public transportation system or an infrastructure facility:

(a) With the intent to cause death or serious bodily injury;

(b) With the intent to cause extensive destruction of such a place, facility or system, where such destruction results in or is likely to result in major economic loss.

2. Any person also commits an offence if that person attempts to commit an offence as set forth in paragraph-1.

3. Any person also commits an offence if that person:

(a) Participates as an accomplice in an offence as set forth in paragraph-1 or 2;

(b) Organises or directs others to commit an offence as set forth in paragraphs-1 or 2;

(c) In any other way contributes to the commission of one or more offences as set forth in paragraphs 1 or 2 by a group of persons acting with a common purpose; such contribution shall be intentional and either be made with the aim of furthering the general criminal activity or purpose of the group or be made in the knowledge of the intention of the group to commit the offence or offences concerned."

Article 2 of the *United Nations International Convention for the Suppression of the Financing of Terrorism, 1999* (Terrorist Financing Convention) defines the crime of terrorist financing as the offence committed by[52]–

"1. Any person commits an offence within the meaning of this Convention, if that person by any means, directly or indirectly, unlawfully and willfully, provides or collects funds with the intention that they should be used or in the knowledge that they are to be used, in full or in part, in order to carry out:

(a) An act which constitutes an offence within the scope of and as defined in one of the treaties listed in the annex; or

(b) Any other act intended to cause death or serious bodily injury to a civilian, or to any other person not taking an active part in the hostilities in a situation of armed conflict, when the purpose of such act, by its nature or context, is to intimidate a population, or to compel a government or an international organisation to do or to abstain from doing any act.

2. On depositing its instrument of ratification, acceptance, approval or accession, a State Party which is not a party to a treaty listed in the annex may declare that, in the application of this Convention to the State Party, the treaty shall be deemed not to be included in the annex referred to in paragraph–1, sub-paragraph,

(a) The declaration shall cease to have effect as soon as the treaty enters into force for the State Party, which shall notify the depositary of this fact;

(b) When a State Party ceases to be a party to a treaty listed in the annex, it may make a declaration as provided for in this article, with respect to that treaty.

3. For an act to constitute an offence set forth in paragraph-1, it shall not be necessary that the funds were actually used to carry out an offence referred to in paragraph-1, sub-paragraphs (a) or (b).

4. Any person also commits an offence if that person attempts to commit an offence as set forth in paragraph-1 of this article.

5. Any person also commits an offence if that person:

(a) Participates as an accomplice in an offence as set forth in paragraphs 1 or 4 of this article;

(b) Organises or directs others to commit an offence as set forth in paragraphs 1 or 4 of this article;

(c) Contributes to the commission of one or more offences as set forth in paragraphs 1 or 4 of this Article by a group of persons acting with a common purpose. Such contribution shall be intentional and shall either:

(i) Be made with the aim of furthering the criminal activity or criminal purpose of the group, where such activity or purpose involves the commission of an offence as set forth in paragraph-1 of this Article;

(ii) Be made in the knowledge of the intention of the group to commit an offence as set forth in paragraph 1 of this Article."

Article 2 of the *United Nations International Convention for the Suppression of Acts of Nuclear Terrorism, 2005* defines the crime of nuclear terrorism as follows[53]–

"1. Any person commits an offence within the meaning of this, Convention if that person unlawfully and intentionally:

(a) Possesses radioactive material or makes or possesses a device:

(i) With the intent to cause death or serious bodily injury;

(ii) With the intent to cause substantial damage to property or to the environment;

(b) Uses in any way radioactive material or a device, or uses or damages a nuclear facility in a manner which releases or risks the release of radioactive material:

(i) With the intent to cause death or serious bodily injury; or

(ii) With the intent to cause substantial damage to property or to the environment; or

(iii) With the intent to compel a natural or legal person, an international organisation or a State to do or refrain from doing an act.

2. Any person also commits an offence if that person:

(a) Threatens, under circumstances which indicate the credibility of the threat, to commit an offence as set forth in paragraph 1(b) of the present Article;

(b) Demands unlawfully and intentionally radioactive material, a device or a nuclear facility by threat, under circumstances which indicate the credibility of the threat, or by use of force.

3. Any person also commits an offence if that person attempts to commit an offence as set forth in paragraph 1 of the present article.

4. Any person also commits an offence if that person:

(a) Participates as an accomplice in an offence as set forth in paragraphs 1, 2 or 3 of the present Article;

(b) Organises or directs others to commit an offence as set forth in paragraphs 1, 2 or 3 of the present Article;

(c) In any other way contributes to the commission of one or more offences as set forth in paragraphs 1, 2 or 3 of the present Article by a group of persons acting with a common purpose; such contribution shall be intentional and either be made with the aim of furthering the general criminal activity or purpose of the group or be made in the knowledge of the intention of the group to commit the offence or offences concerned."

Apart from the above UN Conventions, there are other Regional Conventions formulated at the initiative of various regional organisations to counter the menace of terrorism at the regional levels. This process was started almost at the same time as it was started by the United Nations.

According to Article 1 of *SAARC Regional Convention on Suppression of Terrorism, 1987* subject to the overall requirements of the law of extraditions, the following offences, shall be regarded as offence of terrorism - murder, manslaughter, assault causing bodily harm, kidnapping, hostage-taking and offences relating to firearms, weapons, explosives and dangerous substances when used as a means to perpetrate indiscriminate violence involving death or serious bodily injury to persons or serious damage to property. Even an accomplice would be punished for his act.

Article 1 of this Convention says[54] –

"Subject to the overall requirements of the law of extradition, conduct constituting any of the following offences, according to the law of the Contracting State, shall be regarded as terroristic and for the purpose of extradition shall not be regarded as political offence or as an offence connected with a political offence or as an offence inspired by political motives:

(a) An offence within the scope of the *Convention for the Suppression of Unlawful Seizure of Aircraft*, signed at the Hague on December 16, 1970;

(b) An offence within the scope of the *Convention for the Suppression of Unlawful acts against the safety of Civil* Aviation, signed at Montreal on September 23, 1971;

(c) An offence within the scope of the *Convention on the Prevention and Punishment of Crimes* against Internationally Protected Persons, including Diplomatic Agents, signed at New York on December 14, 1973;

(d) An offence within the scope of any Convention to which SAARC Member Sates concerned are parties and which obliges the parties to prosecute or grant extradition;

(e) Murder, manslaughter, assault causing bodily harm, kidnapping, hostage-taking and offences relating to firearms, weapons, explosives and dangerous substances when used as a means to perpetrate indiscriminate violence involving death or serious bodily injury to persons or serious damage to property;

(f) An attempt or conspiracy to commit an offence described in sub-paragraphs (a) to (e), aiding, abetting or counselling the commission of such an offence or participating as an accomplice in the offences so described."

Article 1 of Arab Convention for the Suppression of Terrorism, 1998 defines Terrorism as[55] –

> "Any act or threat of violence, whatever its motives or purposes, that occurs for the advancement of an individual or collective criminal agenda, causing terror among people, causing fear by harming them, or placing their lives, liberty or security in danger, or aiming to cause damage to the environment or to public or private installations or property or to occupy or to seize them, or aiming to jeopardise a national resource."

Article 1 of the said Convention also define 'terrorist offence' as follows[56] –

> "Any offence or attempted offence committed in furtherance of a terrorist objective in any of the Contracting States, or against their nationals, property or interests, that is punishable by their domestic law. The offences stipulated in the following conventions, except where conventions have not been ratified by Contracting States or where offences have been excluded by their legislation, shall also be regarded as terrorist offences:

(a) The Tokyo Convention on offences and Certain Other Acts Committed on Board Aircraft, of 14th September, 1963;

(b) The Hague Convention for the Suppression of Unlawful Seizure of Aircraft, of 16th December, 1970;

(c) The Montreal Convention for the Suppression of Unlawful Acts against the Safety of Civil Aviation, of 23rd September, 1971, and the Protocol thereto of 10th May 1984;

(d) The Convention on the Prevention and Punishment of

Crimes against Internationally Protected Persons, including Diplomatic Agents, of 14th December, 1973;

(e) The International Convention against the Taking of Hostages, of 17th December, 1979;

(f) The provisions of the United Nations Convention on the Law of the Sea, of 1982, relating to piracy on the high seas.

Article 1 of Treaty on Co-operation among the States Members of the Commonwealth of Independent States in Combating Terrorism, 1999 defines terrorism as[57] –

"an illegal act punishable under criminal law committed for the purpose of undermining public safety, influencing decision-making by the authorities or terrorising the population, and taking the form of:

Violence or the threat of violence against natural or juridical persons;

Destroying (damaging) or threatening to destroy (damage) property and other material objects so as to endanger people's lives;

Causing substantial harm to property or the occurrence of other consequences dangerous to society;

Threatening the life of a statesman or public figure for the purpose of putting an end to his State or other public activity or in revenge for such activity;

Attacking a representative of a foreign State or an internationally protected staff member of an international organisation, as well as the business premises or vehicles of internationally protected persons;

Other acts classified as terrorist under the national legislation of the Parties or under universally recognisized international legal instruments aimed at combating terrorism."

Article 1 of Convention of the Organisation of the Islamic Conference on Combating International Terrorism, 1999 has defined terrorism as[58] –

> "any act of violence or threat thereof notwithstanding its motives or intentions perpetrated to carry out an individual or collective criminal plan with the aim of terrorising people or threatening to harm them or imperiling their lives, honour, freedoms, security or rights or exposing the environment or any facility or public or private property to hazards or occupying or seizing them, or endangering a national resource, or international facilities, or threatening the stability, territorial integrity, political unity or sovereignty of independent States."

This Convention further defined the term 'Terrorist crime' as follows[59] –

> 'Any crime executed, started or participated in to realise a terrorist objective in any of the Contracting States or against its nationals, assets or interests or foreign facilities and nationals residing in its territory punishable by its internal law.'

According Article 1 of *OAU Convention on the Prevention and Combating of Terrorism, 1999,* terrorist act means[60] –

(a) any act which is a violation of the criminal laws of a State Party, and which may endanger the life, physical integrity or freedom of, or cause serious injury or death to, any person, any number or group of persons or causes or may cause damage to public or private property, natural resources, environmental or cultural heritage and is calculated or intended to:

(i) intimidate, put in fear, force, coerce or induce any government, body, institution, the general public or any segment thereof, to do or abstain from doing any act, or to adopt or abandon a particular standpoint, or to act according to certain principles; or

(ii) disrupt any public service, the delivery of any essential service to the public or to create a public emergency; or

(iii) create general insurrection in a State.

(b) any promotion, sponsoring, contribution to, command, aid, incitement, encouragement, attempt, threat, conspiracy, organising, or procurement of any person, with the intent to commit any act referred to in paragraph (a) (i) to(iii)."

IX. *Definitions by Non-United Nations Bodies*

The Council of European Union uses a definition of terrorism for legal/official purposes which is set out in Article 1 of its Framework Decision on Combating Terrorism[61]. This provides that terrorist offences are:

"The intentional acts referred to below in points (a) to (i), as defined as offences under national law, which, given their nature or context, may seriously damage a country or an international organisation where committed with the aim of:

- seriously intimidating a population, or
- unduly compelling a Government or international organisation to perform or abstain from performing any act, or
- seriously destabilising or destroying the fundamental political, constitutional, economic or social structures of a country or an international organisation, shall be deemed to be terrorist offences:

(a) attacks upon a person's life which may cause death;

(b) attacks upon the physical integrity of a person;

(c) kidnapping or hostage taking;

(d) causing extensive destruction to a Government or public facility, a transport system, an infrastructure facility, including an information system, a fixed platform located on the continental shelf, a public place or private property likely to endanger human life or result in major economic loss;

(e) seizure of aircraft, ships or other means of public or goods transport;

(f) manufacture, possession, acquisition, transport, supply or use of weapons, explosives or of nuclear, biological or chemical weapons, as well as research into, and development of, biological and chemical weapons;

(g) release of dangerous substances, or causing fires, floods or explosions the effect of which is to endanger human life;

(h) interfering with or disrupting the supply of water, power or any other fundamental natural resource the effect of which is to endanger human life;

(i) threatening to commit any of the acts listed in (a) to (h)."

The Commonwealth Secretariat – an organisation representing the 53 member states of the British Commonwealth has also made model legislation namely '*Draft Model Legislation on Measures to Combat Terrorism*'. It defines 'terrorist act' on the basis of the conventions, resolutions and other prevailing definitions. Two options are present in this Draft relating to definition of terrorist act. According to option 1 of the said Draft 'terrorist act' means[62]–

(1) an act or omission in or outside .... (name of country) which constitutes an offence within the scope of a counter-terrorism convention;

(2) an act or threat of action in or outside .... (name of country) which –

(a) involves serious bodily harm to a person;

(b) involves serious damage to property;

(c) endangers a person's life;

(d) creates a serious risk to the health or safety of the public or a section of the public;

(e) involves the use of firearms or explosives;

(f) involves releasing into the environment or any part thereof or distributing or exposing the public or any part thereof to–

(i) any dangerous, hazardous, radioactive or harmful substance;

(ii) any toxic chemical;

(iii) any microbial or other biological agent or toxin;

(g) is designed or intended to disrupt any computer system or the provision of services directly related to communications infrastructure, banking or financial services, utilities, transportation or other essential infrastructure;

(h) is designed or intended to disrupt the provision of essential emergency services such as police, civil defence or medical services;

(i) involves prejudice to national security or public safety; and is intended, or by its nature and context, may reasonably be regarded as being intended to:

(ii) intimidate the public or a section of the public;

(iii) compel a government or an international organisation to do, or refrain from doing, any act.

(3) an act which –

(a) disrupts any services;

(b) is committed in pursuance of a protest, demonstration or stoppage of work, shall be deemed not to be a terrorist act within the meaning of this definition, so long and so long only as the act is not intended to result in any harm referred to in paragraphs, (a), (b), (c) or (d) of sub-section (2).

According to option 2 of the same Draft 'terrorist act' means[63]–

(1) an act or omission in or outside .... (name of country) which constitutes an offence within the scope of a counter-terrorism convention;

(2) an act or threat of action in or outside......... (name of country) which -

(a) involves serious bodily harm to a person;

(b) involves serious damage to property;

(c) endangers a person's life;

(d) creates a serious risk to the health or safety of the public or a section of the public;

(e) involves the use of firearms or explosives;

(f) involves releasing into the environment or any part thereof or distributing or exposing the public or any part thereof to –

(i) any dangerous, hazardous, radioactive or harmful substance;

(ii) any toxic chemical;

(iii) any microbial or other biological agent or toxin;

(g) is designed or intended to disrupt any computer system or the provision of services directly related to communications infrastructure, banking or financial services, utilities, transportation or other essential infrastructure;

(h) is designed or intended to disrupt the provision of essential emergency services such as police, civil defence or medical services;

(a) involves prejudice to national security or public safety; and is intended, or by its nature and context, may reasonably be regarded as being intended to –

(i) intimidate the public or a section of the public;

(ii) compel a government or an international organisation to do, or refrain from doing, any act,

(iii) is made for the purpose of advancing a political, ideological, or religious cause.

(3) An act which –

(a) disrupts any services;

(b) is committed in pursuance of a protest, demonstration or stoppage of work, shall be deemed not to be a terrorist act within the meaning of this definition, so long and so long only as the act is not intended to result in any harm referred to in paragraphs, (a), (b), (c) or (d) of subsection (2)."

(x) *Definition in Indian Draft Comprehensive Convention on International Terrorism (CCIT)*

In 1996, India presented a draft of a *Comprehensive Convention on International Terrorism (CCIT)* to the Ad Hoc Committee of the UN General Assembly on International Terrorism. The Article 2 of the Convention defining the offence of terrorism covers offences like unlawful seizure of aircraft, unlawful acts against the safety of civil aviation, crimes against internationally protected persons, taking of hostages, threat to maritime navigation and terrorist bombings. It reads as follows[64]–

"1. Any person commits an offence within the meaning of this Convention if that person, by any means, unlawfully and intentionally, does an act intended to cause:

(a) Death or serious bodily injury to any person; or

(b) Serious damage to a State of government facility, a public transportation system, communication system or infrastructure facility with the intent to cause extensive destruction of such a place, facility or system, or where such destruction results or is likely result in major economic loss; when the purpose of such act, by its nature or context, is to intimidate a population or to compel a Government or an international organisation to do or abstain from doing any act.

2. Any person also commits an offence if that person attempts to commit an offence or participates as an accomplice in an offence as set forth in paragraph-1.

3. Any person also commits an offence if that person:

(a) Organises, directs or instigates others to commit an offence as set forth in paragraphs 1 or 2;

(b) Aids, abets, facilitates or counsels the commission of such an offence;

(c) In any other way contributes to the commission of one or more offences referred to in paragraphs 1, 2 or 3(a) by a group of persons acting with a common purpose; such contribution shall be intentional and either be made with the aim of furthering the general criminal activity or purpose of the group or be made in the knowledge of the intention of the group to commit the offence or offences concerned.

(xi) *Definitions in Indian Statutes and in Various Judicial Decisions*

The Indian Penal Code of 1860, as amended from time to time does not define the term terrorism as an offence; the first special law which attempted to define terrorism was the *Terrorist and Disruptive Activities (Prevention) Act, (TADA)* 1987, which was followed by the *Prevention of Terrorism Act, (POTA) 2002*. In the year 2004, when POTA was repealed, then the *Unlawful Activities (Prevention) Act, 1967* was amended to include the definition of a 'terrorist act'.

For the first time, in the Terrorist Affected Areas (Special

Courts) Act, 1984 which was passed for introducing Special Court to deal with terrorist offences, definition of 'terrorist' is given. According to this Act, 'terrorist' means[65]–

"a person who indulges in wanton killing of persons or in violence or in the disruption of services or means of communications essential to the community or in damaging property with a view to -

(i) putting the public or any section of the public in fear; or

(ii) affecting adversely the harmony between different religious, racial, language or regional groups or castes or communities; or

(iii) coercing or overawing the Government established by law; or

(iv) endangering the sovereignty and integrity of India."

In the wake of the assassination of Prime Minister Indira Gandhi, the *Terrorist and Disruptive Activities (Prevention) Act (TADA)*, 1985 was passed in the year 1985. This Act does not define who a 'terrorist' is but defines a 'terrorist act' as follows[66]–

> "Whoever with intent to overawe the Government as by law established or to strike terror in the people or any section of people or alienate any section of the people or to adversely affect the harmony amongst different sections of the people does any act or thing by using bombs, dynamite or other explosive substances or inflammable substances or firearms or other lethal weapons or poisons or noxious gases or other chemicals or any other substances (whether biological or otherwise) of a hazardous nature in such manner as to cause, or as is likely to cause, death of, or injuries to, any person or persons or damage to, or destruction of property or disruption of any supplies or services essential to the life of the community, commits a terrorist act".

The Indian National Security Guard Act, 1986, defines a `Terrorist' as follows[67]–

"Terrorist means any person, who with intent to overawe the Government as by law established or to strike terror in the people or any section of the people, does any act or thing by using bomb, dynamite or other explosive substance or inflammable substances or firearms or other lethal weapons or poisons or noxious gases or other substances (whether biological or otherwise) of a hazardous nature, in such a manner as to cause or as is likely to cause, death or injuries to any person or persons or damage to or destruction of property, or disruption of any supplies or services essential to the life of community."

After the lapse of TADA in the year 1995, Parliament enacted the *Prevention of Terrorism Act (POTA), 2002*. The definition of terrorism used in TADA was reused and broadened in POTA. According to this Act 'terrorist act' defined as[68] –

"(1) Whoever –

(a) with intent to threaten the unity, integrity, security or sovereignty of India or to strike terror in the people or any section of the people does any act or thing by using bombs, dynamite or other explosive substances or inflammable substances or firearms or other lethal weapons or poisons or noxious gases or other chemicals or by any other substances (whether biological or otherwise) of a hazardous nature or by any other means whatsoever, in such a manner as to cause, or likely to cause, death of, or injuries to any person or persons or loss of, or damage to, or destruction of, property or disruption of any supplies or services essential to the life of the community or causes damage or destruction of any property or equipment used or intended to be used for the defence of India or in connection with any other purposes of the Government of India, any State Government or any of their agencies, or detains any person and threatens to kill or injure such person in order to compel the Government or any other person to do or abstain from doing any act;

(b) is or continues to be a member of an association declared unlawful under the *Unlawful Activities (Prevention) Act*, 1967 (37 of 1967), or voluntarily does an act aiding or promoting in any manner the objects of such association and in either case is in possession of any unlicensed firearms, ammunition, explosive or other instrument or substance capable of causing mass destruction and commits any act resulting in loss of human life or grievous injury to any person or causes significant damage to any property, commits a terrorist act.

Explanation - For the purposes of this sub-section, "a terrorist act" shall include the act of raising funds intended for the purpose of terrorism.

After the repeal of *POTA, 2002* the definition given in this Act was adopted in the *Unlawful Activities (Prevention) Amendment Act, 2004*. This Act defines 'terrorist act' as follows[69] –

"Whoever, with intent to threaten the unity, integrity, security or sovereignty of India or to strike terror in the people or any section of the people in India or in any foreign country, does any act by using bombs, dynamite or other explosive substances or inflammable substances or firearms or other lethal weapons or poisons or noxious gases or other chemicals or by any other substances (whether biological or otherwise) of a hazardous nature, in such a manner as to cause, or likely to cause, death of, or injuries to any person or persons or loss of, or damage to, or destruction of, property or disruption of any supplies or services essential to the life of the community in India or in any foreign country or causes damage or destruction of any property or equipment used or intended to be used for the defence of India or in connection with any other purposes of the Government of India, any State Government or any of their agencies, or detains any person and threatens to kill or injure such person in order to compel the Government in India or the Government of a foreign country or any other person to do or abstain from doing any act, commits a terrorist act."

Again in the year 2008, the Unlawful Activities (Prevention) Amendment Act, 2008 was passed. This Act further defines 'terrorist act' as follows[70] –

"Whoever does any act with intent to threaten or likely to

threaten the unity, integrity, security or sovereignty of India or with intent to strike terror or likely to strike terror in the people or any section of the people in India or in any foreign country,

(a) by using bombs, dynamite or other explosive substances or inflammable substances or firearms or other lethal weapons or poisonous or noxious gases or other chemicals or by any other substances (whether biological radioactive, nuclear or otherwise) of a hazardous nature or by any other means of whatever nature to cause or likely to cause –

(i) death of, or injuries to, any person or persons; or

(ii) loss of, or damage to, or destruction of, property; or

(iii) disruption of any supplies or services essential to the life of the community in India or in any foreign country; or

(iv) damage or destruction of any property in India or in a foreign country used or intended to be used for the defence of India or in connection with any other purposes of the Government of India, any State Government or any of their agencies; or

(b) overawes by means of criminal force or the show of criminal force or attempts to do so or causes death of any public functionary or attempts to cause death of any public functionary; or

(c) detains, kidnaps or abducts any person and threatens to kill or injure such person or does any other act in order to compel the Government of India, any State Government or the Government of a foreign country or any other person to do or abstain from doing any act, commits a terrorist act.

Explanation - For the purpose of this section, public functionary means the constitutional authorities and any other functionary notified in the Official Gazette by the Central Government as a public functionary.

Later the Unlawful Activities (Prevention) Amendment Act, 2012 was passed and this Act received the assent of the President on 03.01. 2013[71]. This Act further amended the definition of 'terrorist act.' Now, the definition of 'terrorist act' according to the *Unlawful Activities (Prevention) Act, 1967* is as follows[72]–

(1) "Whoever does any act with intent to threaten or likely to threaten the unity, integrity, security, economic security or sovereignty of India or with intent to strike terror or likely to strike terror in the people or any section of the people in India or in any foreign country,

(d) by using bombs, dynamite or other explosive substances or inflammable substances or firearms or other lethal weapons or poisonous or noxious gases or other chemicals or by any other substances (whether biological radioactive, nuclear or otherwise) of a hazardous nature or by any other means of whatever nature to cause or likely to cause –

(v) death of, or injuries to, any person or persons; or

(vi) loss of, or damage to, or destruction of, property; or

(vii) disruption of any supplies or services essential to the life of the community in India or in any foreign country; or

(viii) damage to, the monetary stability of India by way of production or smuggling or circulation of high quality counterfeit Indian paper currency, coin or of any other material; or

(viii) damage or destruction of any property in India or in a foreign country used or intended to be used for the defence of India or in connection with any other purposes of the Government of India, any State Government or any of their agencies; or

(e) overawes by means of criminal force or the show of criminal force or attempts to do so or causes death of any public functionary or attempts to cause death of any public functionary; or

(f) detains, kidnaps or abducts any person and threatens to kill or injure such person or does any other act in order to compel the Government of India, any State Government or the Government of a foreign country or an international or inter-governmental organisation or any other person or to do or abstain from doing any act; commits a terrorist act.

Explanation – For the purpose of this section,

(a) Public functionary means the constitutional authorities and any other functionary notified in the Official Gazette by the Central Government as a public functionary.

(b) High quality counterfeit Indian Currency means the counterfeit currency as may be declared after examination by an authorised or notified forensic authority that such currency imitates or compromises with the key security features as specified in the Third Schedule.

(2) The terrorist act includes an act which constitutes an offence within the scope of, and as defined in any of the treaties specified in the Second Schedule."

The definition of 'terrorist act' as given in TADA was scrutinised and upheld by the Supreme Court in the *Kartar Singh v State of Punjab*[73].

In the *Rajiv Gandhi assassination case*[74] the Apex Court had come to the conclusion that this was not a terrorist act under TADA and the accused were sentenced for murder under Sectión 302 read with Section 120B IPC. While the provisions of the *Terrorist and Disruptive Activities (Prevention) Act, 1987* have generally been described as being harsh, none of these could be applied to the perpetrators of the act as the Apex Court held that neither was it a terrorist act u/s 3(1) nor were the activities of the perpetrators 'disruptive' u/s 4 of the TADA Act. The Supreme Court observed the followings –

> "Under Section 3 of TADA in order, there is a terrorist act three essential conditions must be present and these are contained in Sub-section (1) of Section 3 - (1) criminal activity must be committed with the requisite intention or motive, (2) weapons must have been used, and (3) consequence must have ensued."

The Supreme Court in *Hitendra Vishnu Thakur v. State of Maharashtra*[75] held that

> "Terrorism is one of the manifestations of increased lawlessness and cult of violence. Violence and crime constitute a threat to an established order and are a revolt against a civilised society. 'Terrorism' has not been defined

under Terrorist and Disruptive Activities (Prevention) Act (TADA) nor is it possible to give a precise definition of 'terrorism' or lay down what constitutes 'terrorism'. It may be possible to describe it as use of violence when it's most important result is not merely the physical and mental damage of the victim but the prolonged psychological effect it produces or has the potential of producing on the society as a whole. There may be death, injury, or destruction of property or even deprivation of individual liberty in the process but the extent and reach of the intended terrorist activity travels beyond the effect of an ordinary crime capable of being punished under the ordinary penal law of the land and its main objective is to overawe the Government or disturb harmony of the society or 'terrorise' people and the society and not only those directly assaulted, with a view to disturb even tempo, peace and tranquillity of the society and create a sense of fear and insecurity. A terrorist activity does not merely arise by causing disturbance of law and order or of public order. The fallout of the intended activity must be such that it travels beyond the capacity of the ordinary law enforcement agencies to tackle it under the ordinary penal law. Experience shows that `terrorism' is generally an attempt to acquire or maintain power or control by intimidation, and causing fear and helplessness in the minds of the people at large or any Section thereof and is a totally abnormal phenomenon. What distinguishes 'terrorism' from other forms of violence therefore appears to be the deliberate and systematic use of coercive intimidation."

The Supreme Court in *Mohd. Iqbal M. Shaikh v. State of Maharashtra*[76] further held that

> "...it is not possible to give a precise definition of terrorism or to lay down what constitutes terrorism, But... it may be possible to describe it as a use of violence when its most important result is not merely the physical and mental damage of the victim, but the prolonged psychological effect it produces or has the potential of producing on the society as

> a whole. ... if the object of the activity is to disturb harmony of the society or to terrorise people and the society, with a view to disturb even tempo, tranquility of the society, and a sense of fear and insecurity is created in the minds of a section of society at large, then it will, undoubtedly be held to be terrorist act..."

An Overall Discussion over definitions

(i) *Definition of Different States*

Two minor amendments have since been made to the UK definition. The first was made by Section 34 of the *Terrorism Act 2006*, which amended Sub-section (1) (b) to include – government or international governmental organisation. This was inserted to remove the disparity between the original UK definition and other definitions of terrorism in international instruments, such as the *International Convention for the Suppression of the Financing of Terrorism, 1999* and to enable the definition to be applied to acts of terrorism against international bodies, such as the United Nations. The second amendment was made by Section 75 of the *Counter-Terrorism Act 2008*,[77] which amended Sub-section (1)(c) to include acts committed for the purpose of advancing a racial cause and accordingly after "religious" the word "racial" was inserted.

There are a number of general similarities between the Canadian Criminal Code and the '*UK's Terrorism Act* 2000 definitions. These similarities reveal the heavy reliance of the Canadian government on the earlier UK legislation.

First, both definitions include a requirement that the act be committed for the purpose of advancing a political, religious, or ideological cause.

Second, both definitions include reference to acts directed at governments and international organisations, and acts intended to intimidate a section of the public.

Third, both definitions include a list of enumerated harms that extend beyond death or serious bodily injury to property damage, interference with infrastructure, and acts that create a serious risk to the health or safety of a section of the public.

The number of important differences between the Canadian and the UK definitions, however, are more notable.

First, Sub-section (i)(B) of the Canadian definition imposes a higher standard of fault than its UK counterpart by requiring that an act be intended to "compel" its target to act in a particular way. This is a higher standard than the comparable *Terrorism Act 2000* Sub-section (1)(b), which requires that an act be intended to "merely" influence a government or international governmental organisation.

Second, Sub-section (i)(B) of the *Anti-Terrorism Act* definition covers a wider range of potential targets than the *Terrorism Act*, 2000 definition. It extends beyond acts directed at governments, international organisations, and sections of the public to acts directed at domestic organisations and individual persons. That provision also refers to "economic security," which is not mentioned in the UK definition. Third, Sub-section (E) of the Canadian definition contains an exemption for acts of political protest.

There are also several differences between the lists of harms in both definitions. Unlike the UK definition, the list of harms in the Canadian definition refers to "death" and "serious bodily harm". The Canadian list does not refer to acts that merely involve "serious violence against a person." The Canadian list sets a higher threshold for property damage, by requiring that a terrorist act against property result in one of the harms listed in Sub-sections (A)-(C) (unlike the *Terrorism Act 2000* Sub-section (2)(b), which only requires "serious property damage"). Sub-section (E) of the Canadian list extends beyond acts that interfere with "systems" to acts that disrupt "facilities" and "services."

The Australian definition of a terrorist act is broadly similar to its UK and Canadian counterparts, but it also includes a number of unique features. Similar to the UK and Canadian definitions, it requires that the act be committed for the purpose of advancing a political, religious or ideological cause. It also extends to acts that endanger life, create a serious risk to the health or safety of the public, cause property damage, or seriously interfere with electronic systems. Like the United Kingdom's definition, and unlike Canada's definition, acts causing property or electronic damage do not need to also cause death, endanger the life of any person, or create a serious risk to the health or safety of the public. On the other hand, similar to Canada's definition, and unlike the United

Kingdom's definition, Section 100.1(3) provides an exemption for acts of political protest that only intend to cause property damage. In terms of the level of intent required in Sub-section (c)(i), the Australian legislation sits somewhere between the UK and Canadian definitions ("influence" and "compel" respectively) by requiring that the act be committed against a government with the intent of "influencing by intimidation." Sub-section (c)(i) of the Australian definition does not extend to acts committed against international organisations, domestic organisations or individual persons.

The New Zealand Terrorism Suppression Act, 2002 definition appears to be the most restrained. Section 5(2) similarly requires that the act be motivated by a political, religious or ideological cause, but the fault requirements in Sub-sections (2)(a) and (b) set significantly higher standards than the other jurisdictions. Instead of requiring intent to "intimidate" a section of the population (as in the UK, Canadian, and Australian definitions) Sub-section (2)(a) requires intent to "induce terror." This seems to indicate that the act must generate a feeling of intense fear or dread in the population, as opposed to the less emotive "intimidate," which would likely be satisfied by "the use of threats or violence to force to or to restrain from some action." Similarly, Sub-section (2)(b) sets a higher threshold by not merely requiring that the act be designed to "influence," "influence by intimidation," or even "compel" a government or international organisation. Instead, it requires that an act "unduly compel or force" a government or international organisation to do or to abstain from doing any act. Moreover, the list of enumerated harms in Section 5(3) sets higher standards than comparable provisions in the other jurisdictions discussed. Unlike the UK, Australian, Canadian, and South African definitions, Section 5 does not extend to acts that merely "endanger life." Any property damage must be likely to result in death, serious bodily injury, or a serious risk to health or safety. Any interference with infrastructure must be likely to endanger life.

The definition of USA has some similarities to the other definitions as mentioned above.

First, they refer to acts that intend to "intimidate or coerce a civilian population."

Second, they refer to acts that are intended to "influence the policy of a government by intimidation or coercion." This is closest to the Australian definition, which similarly sits between the UK "influence" and the Canadian "compel."

There are, however, a number of differences between the US definitions and the other definitions of terrorism as mentioned above.

First, and most obviously, section 2331 is divided into acts that occur primarily outside and those that occur primarily inside the United States. The other definitions discussed above apply singularly to any acts committed inside or outside the territory of a state.

Second, Section 2331 is not directed at acts with only a political, religious, or ideological cause. Instead, Sub-sections (1)(A) and (5)(A) require that the conduct must be an independent criminal offense which involves violence or is likely to endanger life.

Third, Sub-sections (1)(B)(iii) and (5)(B)(iii) include conduct that merely "affects" the conduct of a government by mass destruction, assassination, or kidnapping."

Lastly, neither of the definitions in Section 2331 provides a basis for prosecuting acts of terrorism under federal law. Instead, these definitions were enacted for the limited purpose of seeking court orders and search warrants against individuals suspected of engaging in terrorist activity. Section 219 of the *USA Patriot Act*, for example, gives federal magistrates in any district the power to issue a nation-wide search warrant for individuals suspected of international or domestic terrorism.

Section 2332(b) defines the crime of "acts of terrorism transcending national boundaries." It lists a range of penalties, ranging from the death penalty or life imprisonment for acts resulting in death, to a maximum of 35 years imprisonment for maiming, 25 years for acts against property, and 10 years for a threat to commit an offence. This is a notable improvement on the other definitions of terrorism discussed above. Rather than being finely calibrated in this way (considering the level of harm caused by an attack), definitions of terrorism in the United Kingdom, Canada, and the other jurisdictions discussed fix a maximum penalty of life imprisonment for any act which qualifies under the provision.

The definition of United States Law Code in title 22 and chapter 38 is inadequate for several reasons.

First, this definition makes no reference to the illegality of politically motivated acts of violence such as murder and kidnapping of civilians. Another important problem with this definition is that it defines terrorism in terms of the victim (non-combatants) instead of the perpetrators and their motives.

If we compare the definitions of terrorism in United States Law and French Law, we can see that United States Law does not list particular acts as terrorist acts; whereas the French law specifically names and describes the acts that constitute terrorism. The definitions of terrorism given in the Acts of different countries almost contain the five basic elements. But in some Acts, list of specific terrorist acts, which can be classified as criminal, is absent. The advantage of not listing specific acts as terrorist acts is that as new forms of technology are created, new forms of terrorist acts are likely to develop, and this law will still cover these news modalities. The disadvantage of not listing specific acts as terrorist acts is that the decision will be left up to policy makers to determine who is and who is not committing terrorist acts. A subjective definition leaves too much room for political bias to affect the decision.

(ii) *Definitions of Different Scholars and Experts*

Schmid found that scholars in the field tend to prefer their own definitions to those of others – in a response to the survey question Whose definition of 'terrorism' do you utilise?– more than half answered 'their own' (58 per cent). The remaining part (42 per cent) favoured a variety of definitions, none of which would gain a particular prominence in being listed significantly more than others.[78]

It seems that Schmid made a sincere effort to construct a definition of terrorism, but his definition could not resolve the following issues:

(i) The boundary between terrorism and other forms of political violence;

(ii) Whether government terrorism and terrorism from below (resistance terrorism) are part of the same phenomenon;

(iii) Separating 'terrorism' from simple criminal acts, from open war between 'consenting' groups and from acts that clearly arise out of mental illness;

(iv) The relation between guerrilla warfare and terrorism; and

(v) Can terrorism be legitimate?

But Schmid overlooked motivation factor, which makes terrorism unique among all other violent acts. Another thing is that, Schmid places agitational terror and enforcement terror at par in his definition, but the reasons and effects of the two are so different that both cannot be considered from an equal platform. The reasons for enforcement terror can never be idiosyncratic or criminal in nature, and it never selects indirect or symbolic targets.

The definition given by Bassiouni does not specifically include the element of intent. However, as the act is conceived of as a strategy, which requires a mental process, the intent element is presumed. Moreover, the term designed to inspire terror evokes the pre-meditated intent of the actor. If the element of intent were absent from this definition, one could presumably be condemned as a terrorist if, in the course of a carefully conducted attack not specifically intended to produce fear and not specifically targetted at innocent civilians, the bomb blast did, in fact, cause fear in the population and cause the accidental injury of one or two civilians. The element of intent should be a necessary requirement in the definition of terrorism in order to permit justifiable attempts at self-defence not involving intentional terrorist acts.

Bassiouni's definition also does not include the targetting of innocent civilians but refers, instead, to a particular segment of a given society. This broad designation of a particular segment of the population could include the military, especially if acts of international terrorism are claimed to arise in the context of a conventional war or armed conflict of an international or of a non-international character. He has given a list of fourteen specific acts of terrorism[79] – such as, aggression, war crimes, crimes against humanity, genocide, apartheid, unlawful human experimentation; torture, slavery and slave-related practices; piracy, and unlawful acts against the safety of maritime navigation; kidnapping of diplomats and other internationally protected persons; taking civilian hostages; serious environmental damage; or serious violation of fundamental human rights. The advantage of this specific listing is the establishment of clarity and certainty in the law. However, the disadvantages are important to recognise. New forms of terrorist acts that develop with the advancement of technology, such as computer hacking, are not specifically included and may fall afoul of the definition. However, this list is very broad and seems to cover the unanticipated act of terrorism under such umbrella categories as aggression, or serious violation of fundamental human rights. Absent from this list, however, is the use of weapons of mass destruction which will necessarily, if not intentionally, inflict harm on innocent civilians.

Bassiouni also mentioned the obstacles to give a comprehensive definition of terrorism. According to him[80] –

> "To define 'terrorism' in a way that is both all-inclusive and unambiguous is very difficult, if not impossible. One of the principal difficulties lies in the fundamental values at stake in the acceptance or rejection of terror-inspiring violence as means of accomplishing a given goal. The obvious and well-known ranges of views on these issues are what makes an internationally accepted specific definition of what is loosely called "terrorism," a largely impossible undertaking. That is why the search for and internationally agreed upon definition may well be a futile and unnecessary effort."

(iii) *Definition in International Law Commission*

The International Law Commission considered terrorism when drafting its 1954 *Draft Code of Offences against the Peace and Security of Mankind (Part I)*.[81] Although, the 1954 ILC Draft Code was never formally adopted by the General Assembly. According to Article 2(6) an offence 'against the peace and security of mankind' is the undertaking or encouragement by the authorities of a State of terrorist activities in another State, or the toleration by the authorities of a State of organised activities calculated to carry out terrorist acts in another State. After the postponement of 1954, the ILC resumed consideration of the *Draft Code in 1982*, when the General Assembly invites the ILC to resume its work relating to the *offences against the Peace and Security of Mankind* by its resolution 36/100.[82] Following nine reports by a Special Rapporteur between 1983 and 1991, the ILC adopted a first reading of a Draft Code in the year 1991.

Article 24 of the *1991 ILC Draft Code*, based on Article 2(6) of the *1954 Draft Code*, proposed an offence where a State agent or representative commits or orders the following things, such as -- undertaking, organising, assisting, financing, encouraging or tolerating acts against another State directed at persons or property and of such a nature as to create a state of terror in the minds of public figures, groups of persons or the general public.[83] Compared with the 1954 draft, this provision partially incorporates the 1937 League definition; added the notions of 'organising', 'assisting' and 'financing'; and included an express reference to acts against property. In 1995, a renumbered draft Article 24 retained similar wording to the 1991 draft, but added that acts must be committed 'in order to compel' the victim State 'to grant advantages or to act in a specific way.'[84] The final *ILC Draft Code (Part II)* was adopted in 1996.[85] While earlier drafts between 1990 and 1995 had included distinct articles on 'international terrorism', a discrete terrorist offence was subsumed by, and recast within, final Article 20 on 'war crimes'.[86]

IV. *Definitions in UN General Assembly and Security Council Resolutions*

The United Nations Organisation has been unable to reach a decision on the definition of terrorism exactly because of these conflicting interests of sovereign states that determine in each and every instance how a particular armed movement (i.e., a non-state actor) is labelled in regard to the terrorist-freedom fighter dichotomy.

The definition given in the resolutions of General Assembly relating to "Measures to eliminate international terrorism" requires *mens rea* with respect to the criminal act's consequences and excludes any possible justification for the act. Resolutions of the General Assembly do not make law *per se*, although they can evidence the opinions of states and be declarative of law. In certain basic aspects, this description resembles the language of the League of Nations draft convention of 1937.

Although Resolution 1373 of the Security Council mandates that member states take serious action to counter terrorism, it lacks a definition of terrorism that would establish the parameters for the implementation of counter-terrorism efforts. The term terrorism described in resolution 1566 of the Security Council appeared to be a definition of terrorism. According to a Security Council press release,[87]

Ambassador Ronaldo Mota Sardenberg of Brazil stated to the Security Council during its debate of *Resolution 1566* that operative paragraph 3 was not an attempt to define the concept of terrorism but rather a compromise among the Member States that contained a clear political message. But over time, paragraph 3 is likely to be recognised as the Security Council's definition of terrorism, *de facto,* if not *de jure.* It is important to note, however, that the definition is qualified by the phrase "which constitute offences within the scope of and as defined in the international conventions and protocols relating to terrorism." Thus, the most significant of the Security Council statements on terrorism can be read to support the notion that terrorism is the aggregate of the existing definitions of terrorism in the conventions. *Resolution 1566* avoids the contentious issue of whether military targets can be the subject of terrorist attacks by defining the class of victims as "including . . . civilians," thereby implying further targets fall within the definition. Such targets might include political and state leaders, depending on, who is regarded as a civilian, but most likely provides plausible grounds for arguing that the definition includes attacks on military targets as acts of terrorism. Irrespective of the intention of the Security Council and whether the definition is exhaustive or otherwise, *Resolution 1566's* definition is an important pronouncement and should be read as partially filling the gap in *Resolution 1373.* The pronouncement, however, remains subject to the legitimate criticism that because it endorses a definition of terrorism ascertainable from the conventions, it adds little new to the development of terrorism as a legal concept. Nevertheless, *Resolution 1566*, although not of law-making force, goes some way to clarifying the extent of the obligations in Resolution 1373, and, for this reason, it is significant.

Terrorism was not defined in resolutions after 11 September; nor were lists of terrorists established, although the *CTC* blithely encouraged States to use lists to "eliminate the need for proof of actual involvement" in terrorism. The CTC also decided not to define terrorism, "although its members had a fair idea of what was blatant terrorism".

Instead, the CTC proposed an ad hoc approach, deciding whether an act is terrorism "where necessary" and referring political controversies to the Council or other bodies. Its mandate is based on a pragmatic view that terrorism can be combated even without agreement on its criminal wrongfulness in all situations. *Resolution 1373* was, however, drafted partly on the basis that the sectoral treaties provided a framework definition. Even so, the CTC has openly allowed States to unilaterally define terrorist acts. While flexibility in implementation is warranted due to variations in domestic legal systems, this effectively means that each State unilaterally defines terrorism, without any outer legal boundaries set by the international community. Far from urging States to confine overly broad legislation, the CTC has advocated that domestic terrorism laws be jurisdictionally widened to cover international terrorism, even though some domestic crimes more closely resemble broad national security or public order offences. The failure to define terrorism has provoked mixed reactions from Council members. Colombia believed that definition was unnecessary, since terrorism was defined in *Assembly Resolution 49/60*. Whereas Mauritius did not want to "quibble" about definition,[88] other States have placed more value on it.[89] Syria stated that non-definition had encouraged violations of human rights and IHL, and encouraged "selective accusations of terrorism".[90]

The *Resolution 1566* also created a working group to report on measures that could be imposed on individuals, groups or entities involved in, or associated with, terrorist activities, other than those designated by the 1267 committee.[91] The definition of "terrorism" provides explicit guidance to States (and the working group and *CTC*) on the meaning of terrorism, and may also exert pressure in the General Assembly to break the impasse on the *Draft Comprehensive Convention*. It presents a relatively narrow definition, limited to acts constituting sectoral offences (typically serious violence endangering life or property, and requiring an international element), which are also intended to create terror, intimidate a population, or coerce a government or organisation. It thus combines elements of the definitions in the General Assembly's 1994 *Declaration on Measures to Eliminate International Terrorism*,[92] and the *International Convention for the Suppression of the Financing of Terrorism, 1999*. It is, however, at variance with the definitions proposed in Art. 2(1) of the current *Draft Comprehensive Convention* and by the UN High-Level Panel in late 2004. While both of those proposals refer to intimidation and coercion (as in *SC Resolution 1566*), neither of the proposed definitions covers acts aimed solely to provoke terror. The definition in *Resolution 1566* does not require a political or other motive, thus encompassing private acts which terrorise, intimidate or coerce. Consequently, some of the distinctiveness of terrorism, as political violence, is lost. Pragmatically, the definition may be too little, too late. In the three years to 2004, many States adopted laws implementing their obligations, and it is unlikely that they will further reform their laws to limit "terrorism" in conformity with the *Resolution* (which merely "recalls" that certain acts are never justified and does not require law reform). As discussed earlier, there are also legitimacy costs in circumventing the treaty process. In 2006, the *Special Rapporteur on Counter-Terrorism*, Scheinin, expressed his support to the United Nations Commission on Human Rights for the 'indispensable' definition of terrorism outlined in *Resolution 1566.*[93]

The international community is still paralysed by rivalries and power struggles among United Nations member states over the issue of definition of the term and eventual exemptions from its application. In the present unipolar system, it has become even more difficult to resolve the underlying conflicts of interest between member states. The central – and yet unresolved -- question is still – Who has the "power of definition"? As long as there is no answer to this question and as long as the proposals advanced by legal theory cannot be reconciled with the conflicting interests of member states, the United Nations Organisation will be incapable of adopting an efficient multilateral approach in the struggle against terrorism.

(v) *Definitions by Different United Nations Conventions and other Conventions*

None of the conventions contain a comprehensive definition of the term terrorism. Rather, the conventions are operational in nature and confined to specific subjects, whether air safety, maritime navigation and platforms, the protection of persons, or the suppression of the means by which terrorist acts may be perpetrated or supported. The multilateral conventions are not applicable to state-sponsored terrorism. They apply only to terrorism committed by individual actors. The absence of a universally accepted definition of terrorism and the inapplicability of multilateral anti-terrorism legislation to state-sponsored terrorism reflect the deeply political nature of the term terrorism.

Among the international and regional anti-terrorism instruments, eight conventions and two related protocols obligate parties to penalise offences defined in the instrument. They are:

(a) *the Convention for the Suppression of Unlawful Seizure of Aircraft, 1970*;

(b) *the Convention on the Suppression of Unlawful Acts Against the Safety of Civil Aviation, 1971 (Montreal Convention)*;

(c) *the Protocol for the Suppression of Unlawful Acts of Violence at Airports Serving International Civil Aviation, 1988*;

(d) *the Convention on the Prevention and Punishment of Crimes against Internationally Protected Persons Including Diplomatic Agents, 1973*;

(e) *the International Convention against taking Hostages, 1979*;

(f) *the Convention on the Physical Protection of Nuclear Material, 1979*;

(g) *the Convention for the Suppression of Unlawful Acts against the Safety of Maritime Navigation, 1988*;

(h) *protocol to the above mentioned Convention for Suppression of Unlawful Acts Against the Safety of Fixed Platforms Located on the Continental Shelf* ;

(i) *the International Convention for the Suppression of Terrorist Bombing, 1997*;

(j) *the International Convention for the Suppression of the Financing of Terrorism, 1999*.

It was the *International Convention for the Suppression of the Financing of Terrorism, 1999*, which attempted for the first time a definition of international terrorism. It consists of two elements. The first relies on the success of prohibiting specific action in the Conventions that where brought about from the 1960s to the 1980s. Article 2, para 1(a) of the *Convention* simply refers to these specific conventions and declares as terrorism acts which are mentioned in these conventions. The second element is the first abstract definition of terrorism in international law, which is contained in Article 2, para 1(b) of the *convention*. The definition given in the International *Convention for the Suppression of the Financing of Terrorism, 1999* does not specifically refers to acts of violence but refers, instead, to criminal acts. The definition arguably includes the element of targetting innocent civilians in the term general public. It includes the element of intent by the words intended or calculated to provoke. The requirement of coercion or intimidation is included in the term terror. However, this definition does not include state-sponsored actors. Moreover, the definition expands the motivation of terrorism to almost any possible cause, other than military. The definition does convey very clearly that the root cause or motivation of the terrorist act does not provide any justification whatsoever for terrorism.

This Convention expressly excludes reference to political motives as a jurisdiction for terrorist acts. However, the Convention does not address the issue of state terrorism. The definition given makes no reference to possible perpetrators and additionally the preamble takes up the wording of the *General Assembly resolution 51/210 of 1996,* condemning terrorist acts by whoever committed. This leads to the conclusion, that in principle, states are under an obligation to apply the provisions concerning the drying out of financial resources also with respect to state terrorism, if it has the "international" element required by Articles 3 and 7 of the Conventions.

The International Convention for the Suppression of Terrorist Bombing, 1997 was the first agreement to use the word "terrorist" in its title as well as in the preamble. In Article 5, it also required the adoption of measures to ensure that offences created by the Convention, "in particular where they are intended or calculated to provoke a state of terror in the general public or in a group of persons or particular persons, are under no circumstances justifiable by considerations of a political, philosophical, ideological, racial, ethnic, religious or other similar nature and are punished by penalties consistent with their grave nature." *The International Convention for the Suppression of the Financing of Terrorism, 1999 and the International Convention for the Suppression of Acts of Nuclear Terrorism, 2005* closely resemble the *Terrorist Bombing Convention* by their use of the terrorism terminology in their titles, preambles and in articles specifying that no justification may be permitted for acts of terrorism. But none of these instruments use the word terrorism or terrorist in their offence definitions. Those definitions employ only traditional criminal code terminology a description of an act constituting a social harm, such as bombing, hostage-taking or use of a ship to distribute dangerous materials, and a general or specific illegal intent, without any requirement that terrorism be mentioned or defined.

The definition of terrorism offered by the *Security Council in Resolution 1566* is strikingly similar to Article 2(1) of the *Financing Convention*. Adopted by the Security Council in 2004, *Resolution 1566* called for increased international co-operation in the fight against terrorism. It called upon states to become parties to the relevant international conventions and protocols, to resolve all obstacles to drafting an international convention on terrorism, and to 'intensify their interaction' with the United Nations[94]. It also called upon states to deny safe haven to any person who supports a terrorist act, facilitates a terrorist act, or harbours a terrorist suspect[95]. *Resolution 1566* was enacted under the Security Council's Chapter VII mandatory powers, but it did not expressly require that Member States adopt the definition of terrorism that it offered in Article 3. The Financing Convention calls upon states to establish appropriate criminal penalties for any person who 'by any means, directly or indirectly, unlawfully and willfully, provides or collects funds with the intention that they should be used or in the knowledge that they are to be used, in full or in part, in order to carry out' a terrorist act[96].

A domestic definition of terrorism should not encompass more conduct than the definitions of terrorism contained in the Financing Convention or *Resolution 1566*, because these represent the best available examples of definitions of terrorism in the international community. But three problems exist with this argument.

First, states are not required to use either definition in domestic criminal legislation. Neither the Financing Convention nor the Resolution 1566 definition is a mandatory definition that states must reflect in domestic law.

Second, there is no absolute international consensus that these represent the best available definitions of terrorism. A range of authoritative sources have supported both definitions, but states still pursue a number of different approaches to defining terrorism in their own criminal legislation.

Thus, the Financing Convention and Resolution 1566 definitions both have strong normative force as examples of how to define terrorism, but they do not provide a definitive standard for assessing whether or not a domestic statutory definition of terrorism is overbroad.

The third problem with relying on the Financing Convention and Resolution 1566 definitions is that, while useful and persuasive, these definitions are not comprehensive. States may look to the Financing Convention and Resolution 1566 for guidance on the appropriate levels of harm and intent to include in a domestic definition of terrorism, but they cannot rely on them to solve a range of other difficult definitional issues. For example, those definitions provide no further guidance to states on whether (or how) to refer to specific types of attacks, such as bio-and cyber terrorism, whether to criminalise state terrorism through domestic legislation. It is possible that a definition of terrorism could include these additional limbs without being overbroad, but the Financing Convention and Resolution 1566 definitions provide no guidance on this issue.

Suffering the lack of a legally binding universal comprehensive definition of international terrorism, we have to stress that such definitions have been elaborated by some regional conventions already. Some of them adopted an easier method, establishing their scope of application by including in their texts the list of universal sectoral conventions or offenses established in these conventions, for example, the European Convention on the Suppression of Terrorism of 1977, as amended by its Protocol of 2003 (Article 1) and the Inter-American Convention Against Terrorism of 2002, (Article 2). Another group of regional conventions -- the Organisation of African Unity Convention on the Prevention and Combating of Terrorism of 1999, (Article 1, paragraph 3) and the Treaty on Co-operation Among the States Members of the Commonwealth of Independent States in Combating Terrorism of 1999, (Article 1) tries to elaborate a substantial comprehensive definition of terrorism or of terrorist acts, describing them with subjective and objective characteristics of criminal acts.

Finally, there are regional conventions of comprehensive character that try to combine the methods of defining *terrorism* applied by two previous categories: the Arab Convention on the Suppression of

Terrorism of 1998, (Article 1); the Convention of the Organisation of the Islamic Conference on Combating International Terrorism of 1999, (Article 1); the original version of the European Convention on the Suppression of Terrorism of 1977, (Article 1); and the South Asian Association for Regional Cooperation Regional Convention on Suppression of Terrorism of 1987, (Article 1). These combined definitions seem to fill up gaps and loopholes in definitions based exclusively on one of the above-mentioned backgrounds.[97]

During the work on the UN convention, the participating States were not able to agree on such basic questions as what the purpose of terrorism is or who can commit terrorism. Ad Hoc Committee established by the General Assembly resolution 51/210 of 17 December, 1996, in its report in the year 2001, submitted that in particular, no consensus had been reached regarding whether a definition should cover State terrorism and where the line is to be drawn between terrorism and legitimate struggles against oppression. Acts of terrorism normally refer to acts committed by non-State actors. However, some argue that acts committed by States may also constitute terrorism (State terrorism) and others argue that some States sponsor terrorism by aiding non-State actors who commit terrorist offences.[98]

An analysis of legislation required in order to meet international counter-terrorism standards is normally the first step to becoming a party to the global terrorism-related conventions and protocols. Governments and legislatures understandably want to know in advance what changes in their legal system will be required as a result of membership in an international treaty or compliance with other international standards. Some countries will not, either because of domestic law or as a matter of policy, adopt a treaty until legislation is in effect that permits the fulfillment of all of its international obligations, and do not consider a treaty binding until implemented by a domestic law. In other countries, adoption of a treaty may automatically incorporate its provisions into domestic law, which would permit articles relating to mutual legal assistance and other procedural matters to serve as self-executing legal authorisation for their use upon the treaty entering into force, without further executive or legislative action except for the practical step of publication of the treaty in the official gazette or otherwise giving notice to the public.

However, even countries that follow what is called a "monist" tradition of automatic treaty incorporation will require legislation to provide non-self executing elements essential to implementation.

The clearest example of this relates to criminalisation of offences. None of the terrorism-related agreements specify a penalty or even a penalty range for the offences defined therein. Typical language is found in Article 4 of the *International Convention for the Suppression of the Financing of Terrorism, 1999.*[99]

"Each State Party shall adopt such measures as may be necessary:

(a) To establish as criminal offences under its domestic law the offences set forth in Article 2;

(b) To make those offences punishable by appropriate penalties which take into account the grave nature of the offences?"

Even if a country's legal tradition were to allow the theoretical possibility of a criminal charge for committing an offence defined only in an international treaty by which that country was bound, and not in a domestic piece of legislation, that offence would remain a crime without punishment until legislation defined the penalty. A fundamental principle of the rule of law is that there can be no punishment without a law, and few persons would argue in favour of allowing punishment to be imposed by analogy to another offence. Consequently, a country that automatically incorporates an offence into its domestic law upon the adoption of a treaty, as defined therein, must take legislative action to provide a penalty for that offence and to implement any other non-self executing provisions.

Rather than enacting special laws on terrorism and creating specific offences of terrorism, some countries prefer to simply amend their Penal Code or Code of Penal Procedure to fill any gaps between existing law and the requirements of particular conventions or protocols. This approach is not precluded by the terrorism-related conventions and protocols, none of which require use of the words "terrorist" or "terrorism" to define prohibited conduct. The word "terrorism" is not found in any of the pertinent conventions from 1963 through 1979, even though historically the agreements were clearly responses to terrorist incidents. The word first appears in the preamble to the *International Convention against taking Hostages, 1979,* referring to the need for co-operation against acts of hostage taking as manifestations of international terrorism, and is repeated in the preambles of subsequent agreements.

(i) Definition in Indian Draft Comprehensive Convention on International Terrorism (CCIT)

At its 53rd Session, the General Assembly decided that the negotiations on the draft *Comprehensive Convention on International Terrorism,* based on the draft circulated by India earlier at the 51st Session in 1996, would commence in the Ad Hoc Committee at its meeting in September 2000. In addition, it would also take up the question of convening a high-level conference under the auspices of the United Nations to address these issues. Since then, the matter has been under active consideration of the Ad Hoc Committee and the Sixth Committee of the UN General Assembly. There is nonetheless a high-degree of understanding that the text of Article 2, prepared by the co-ordinator during the sixth session of the Ad Hoc Committee may serve as a good basis for further considerations of definition problem.[100] According to this Report, the UN draft convention, being simultaneously a comprehensive definition of international terrorism, is actually the most developed and 'all-inclusive' universal definition. As such, it will still require a lot of substantial and 'cosmetic' work from a legal point of view before it will reach its final shape.[101]

A close look at Article 2, would make it clear that it seeks to cover various types of terrorist acts perpetrated "by any means" which might result in death or serious bodily injury and damage or destruction of property including State or government facilities, public transportation systems or infrastructure facilities. Article 2(1)(b) of the *Convention for the suppression of the Financing of Terrorism* is also similar in phraseology.

I. *Definitions in Indian Statutes*

The Indian definition of terrorism is the result of a complicated legislative history involving a number of re-enactments and amendments of earlier anti-terrorism and broader security legislation.

The definition given in the *Terrorist Affected Areas (Special Courts) Act, 1984* was specific about the scope of terrorist targets, but it did not include a motive – that is, it did not explicitly say, for example, 'with intent to secede from India' or 'with a political goal in mind.' Rather, the act mentions what might result from a terrorist act, not what political sentiment motivates the terrorist to commit the crime.

In the *Terrorist and Disruptive Activities (Prevention) Act (TADA), 1985*, the definition of 'terrorist act' is a slight modification of the previous Act. The main difference between TADA and the previous law was the inclusion of an element of 'motive'. Those who drafted TADA believed that any attempt to "strike terror in the people or a section of the people" was in effect an act of terrorism. Any larger or more justifiable reason for causing the terror was irrelevant in so far as the enforcement of the act was concerned. In other words, motive was to be read in the immediate impact of the act itself, not the reasoning behind it.[102] The same principle is embodied in the POTA.

The Second Administrative Reforms Commission was of a different view regarding the observation of Supreme Court in *Rajiv Gandhi assassination case*[103] and believed that the assassination of the former Prime Minister along with 18 other persons was in itself sufficient to conclude that this heinous act was done with a view to strike terror in people. Besides, it had been observed that many a time terrorist outfits target personnel belonging to the security forces or enforcement agencies in order to demoralise them or to avenge any strict action taken by them. The basic purpose behind these acts was to terrorise other personnel from taking action against terrorists. The Commission, therefore, felts that assassination of important public figures, as also murder of public functionaries by way of revenge or with a view to subdue others in the organisation, should be categorised as a terrorist act.[104]

In the definition given in *Prevention of Terrorism Act (POTA), 2002*, motive is also present. This Act was also repealed and the *Unlawful Activities (Prevention) Act, 1967* was amended in the year 2004. The POTA 2002, definition made clear that mere possession of any instrument or substance "capable of causing mass destruction" by members of an unlawful association was included within the definition of a terrorist act, as was the raising of funds "for the purpose of terrorism." Since 2002, this legislation has ostensibly been directed towards the same post-9/11 security environment that justified new legislation in the United Kingdom and the United States. However, for at least the last fifteen years, India has relied upon definitions of terrorism that refer to uncertain and extraordinarily broad forms of harm such as "injuries," the "destruction of property," and the "disruption" of essential services.

A major change in the definition of 'terrorist act' in TADA and POTA was the substitution of *'with intent to overawe the government'* with the phrase *"with intent to threaten the unity, integrity, security or sovereignty of India'*. With this amendment, the definition of 'terrorist act' became more precise. Another major change in the definition of 'terrorist act' in POTA was clause 3(1)(b) which stipulated that being a member of an 'unlawful association' or promoting any such association and possessing substances capable of causing mass destruction and committing any act resulting in loss of human life or grievous injury, would also amount to a 'terrorist act'.

In the *Prevention of Terrorism Act, 2002 (POTA)*, the phrase '*act of raising funds intended for the purpose of terrorism*' was included in the definition of the term *'a terrorist act'* provided in Section 3(1), by way of an Explanation to it.

POTA had contained a paragraph in the definition of a 'terrorist act' which provided that the possession of unlicensed fire arms etc., and commitment of an act resulting in loss of human life or causing damage to property by any member or a supporter of an association declared unlawful under the *Unlawful Activities (Prevention) Act, 1967* was also a 'terrorist act'. This provision was included on the recommendation of the Law Commission of India in its 173rd report on *Prevention of Terrorism Bill, 2000*. The Law Commission had occasion to look at international legislations and it was of the view that the legislation in the United Kingdom defined 'terrorism' and 'terrorist' in more extensive terms.[105]

In *People's Union for Civil Liberties* v. *Union of India,*[106] the constitutional validity of various provisions of POTA was challenged before the Supreme Court. Herein, the Court felt that though it is difficult to explain the phenomenon of terrorism, however a 'terrorist act' is easily identifiable when it does occur and thus the basic meaning of the term is clear. The Court referring the major characteristics of terrorism as set out by Paul Wilkinson, an authority on terrorism related works, mentioned the main characteristics of terrorism, which are as follows –

(1) It is premeditated and aims to create a climate of extreme fear or terror;

(2) It is directed at a wider audience or target than the immediate victims of violence;

(3) It inherently involves attacks on random and symbolic targets, including civilians;

(4) The acts of violence committed are seen by the society in which they occur as extra-normal, in literal sense that they breach the social norms, thus causing a sense of outrage; and

(5) Terrorism is used to influence political behaviour in some way – for example to force opponents into conceding some or all of the perpetrators demands, to provoke an over-reaction, to serve as a catalysis for more general conflict, or to publicise a political cause.

Furthermore, the Court observed that it is the psychological element that distinguishes terrorist acts from political offences and discussed the increase in terrorist activities in recent years, which has led to the need for an Act like POTA.[107]

In order to make the definition more effective, terrorist acts should be delineated with greater specificity. Furthermore, there should be an explicit requirement of intent as an element of all terrorist offences. This would limit the discretion in the hands of authorities and stave off abuse.

POTA has listed out specific crimes in greater detail than either the UK or USA's definitions. However, it subsequently undermined any benefits of specificity of the list of crimes given by following its list with the words "or by any other means whatsoever," which rendered the definition overbroad and invited abuse by allowing for subjectivity and giving a lot of leeway to the authorities in interpretation. Thus, the definition should be made more restrictive and these terms should be deleted.

Furthermore, a *proviso* should be added to the definition that states that a "terrorist act" does not include an act, if such act is lawful advocacy, protest, dissent or industrial action so as to ensure that the fundamental rights of people are protected and civil rights are not infringed upon by the government or officials in the name of national security and personal vendettas. Another addition that has been recommended is the inclusion of the intent to adversely affect the harmony amongst different sections of the people as it existed under TADA within the definition of terrorist act in POTA, as well as this is important in a country as diverse and conflicted as India.

The Second Administrative Reforms Commission feels that including provisions which make the possession of certain arms etc., and commission of certain acts by members or supporters of 'terrorist organisations' a 'terrorist act' would strengthen the law enforcement authorities in their fight against terrorism.[108] However, the Commission feels that although paragraph (b) of Section 3(1) of POTA equated the commission of a 'terrorist act' with an act committed by a member or supporter of a terrorist organisation on possession of certain arms etc., its subjection to the qualifying condition that such an act should result in 'loss of human life or grievous injury to any person' or cause 'significant damage to any property' substantially reduced its intended impact. The Commission is of the considered view that whether such an act results in the loss, injury or damage mentioned above is inconsequential, what is paramount is the commission of the act by members or supporters of terrorist organisations on possession of certain arms etc. Accordingly, paragraph (b) of Section 3(1) under POTA which was not included in the UAPA should be included in the definition of a 'terrorist act' in the proposed new legislation. However, it should cover not only the acts committed by members or supporters of terrorist organisations resulting in 'loss of human life or grievous injury to any person' or causing 'significant damage to any property', but also acts which are likely to cause such death, injury or damage.[109]

Though these Acts have been repealed and hence the definitions given in those Acts are no longer law, however there is greater need to study these definitions and try and improve them so as to ensure a functional, effective and comprehensive definition of terrorism.

The Indian definition does not refer to acts that are intended to influence, intimidate or compel governments or international organisations, but those that are "likely to threaten the unity, integrity, security or sovereignty of India." Like the Canadian definition, the Indian definition includes reference to acts disrupting essential services, although this disruption need not be serious. This broad provision led

Reuven Young to remark that "simply cutting a telephone line would probably not constitute terrorism at international law, but it would in India."[110] Moreover, the Indian definition encompasses mere (as opposed to "serious" or "substantial") property damage, which is unique among the definitions discussed in this article. The inclusion of acts causing "injuries" to persons, as opposed to the higher and more common threshold of "serious bodily harm" is also unique to the Indian definition. The current UAPA definition also recognises specific acts of terrorism such as assassination and kidnapping, which are not included in the other definitions as mentioned above. Along with the reference to "unity, integrity, security and sovereignty," these inclusions probably reflect India's more extensive experience with acts of domestic and separatist violence.

The history of the Indian legislation demonstrates many of the problems with defining terrorism in domestic law. It shows how domestic politico-historical contexts can influence what states believe should amount to terrorist activity. In India's case, this includes a longstanding pre-occupation with issues of secession and territorial sovereignty, as well as acts involving firearms, assassination, and kidnapping. The Indian experience also reveals the possible serious consequences of enacting imprecise and overbroad definitions of terrorism. Perhaps above all, it shows that definitions of terrorism display a remarkable resilience to repeal or atrophy, and, if anything, tend to increase in scope over subsequent iterations. The complicated legislative history of the UAPA amendments, TADA, and POTA 2002 demonstrates the tendency of overbroad definitions of terrorism to become normalised in domestic jurisdictions to the point where they can even re-appear after significant public opposition.

General and Specific Approaches in Defining Terrorism

To define terrorism there are both *general* and *specific* approaches. The *specific* approach identifies certain activities as terrorism, such as hijacking and taking hostages, without seeking to define a general category of terrorism *per se,* while the *general* approach seeks to arrive at a general definition of terrorism, by reference to criteria such as intention, motivation, and so forth. The former is essentially an *inductive* approach, while the latter is *deductive*. These approaches can be combined in one definition.

Almost in all the definitions as mentioned above, most of them have adopted a largely *general* approach. However, some countries' definitions include *specific* elements, such as S.5(1)(b) of the *New Zealand Terrorism Suppression Act, 2002* and para (a) of the definition of 'terrorist activity' in Section 83.01 of the *Canadian Criminal Code*, which provide that certain offences constitute terrorist acts. In addition, there are *specific* elements in Australian legislation, which refer to certain terrorist activities. Even in some Acts terrorism is defined by reference to certain acts against specified terrorism conventions. But it is not clear exactly what an act against a specified terrorist convention would look like. However, a specific offence may not include the elements that distinguish a terrorist act from other criminal acts. Another problem with the specific approach is 'that as new forms of technology are created, new forms of terrorist acts are likely to develop'.[111] A general approach may be needed to cover these new things.[112] This problem may be overcome by enacting an extensive list of specific crimes of terrorism, which may even anticipate new forms of terrorist activity. However, this would pit the legislative drafter and the usually slow and unwieldy parliamentary process against the ingenuity of terrorists seeking new ways to achieve their goals. For that reason, legislative definitions of terrorism based upon specific offences will produce longer statutes that cannot cover the ambit of all possible terrorist action.

Where specific offences of terrorism do not sufficiently cover the field, terrorist conduct may still fall within the ordinary criminal law, including offences such as murder and assault. However, such actions might thereby avoid some of the additional sanctions (such as additional times of imprisonment) often associated with terrorist acts, and may not attract the special investigative and detention powers that many nations have provided for only in regard to the commission of terrorist crimes. Other acts such as cyber terrorism, or even acts not yet dreamed of, may fall entirely outside of the ordinary criminal law. Hence, in my opinion, a specific approach in defining terrorism is not sufficient.

In other case, where attempt has been made to formulate a *general* definition of terrorism, the basic sense of what is meant by 'terrorism' has not proven to be too elusive. In almost all of the definitions of the different countries the concept refers to political, religious or ideologically-motivated violence that causes harm to people or property, intended either to coerce a civilian population or government, or to instil fear in the population or a certain part of it. However, if a definition is expressed at this level of abstraction, it would extend to a range of activities not generally considered to be terrorism. Civil disobedience, public protest and industrial action are among the activities that could fall within the definition. These types of activities should be excluded from any definition of terrorism. The legislation simply requires the purported terrorist to have committed an act (such as endangering a person's life, or seriously damaging property), and to have committed that act in furtherance of a political, religious or ideological cause with the aim of influencing the government or intimidating the public (or a section thereof). This encompasses groups whose methods are generally non-violent and who do not aim to intimidate or to coerce the government or the public.

However, the definition in the Terrorism Act of UK does cover activities such as industrial disputes and mass public demonstrations. Indeed, if this were not the case, it would have been a simple matter to exclude certain categories of acts, such as advocacy, dissent and industrial action. Given the specific exclusion clauses in the Australian, New Zealand and Canadian legislations, the absence of such a clause might even create an implication that Parliament intended to include these acts within the scope of the definition. While we have used the United Kingdom definition to highlight the problems of defining terrorism in a *general*, deductive manner without specific exceptions, the United States definition could produce similar results. It also lacks an appropriate exception clause.

The principal disadvantage of generic definition is the difficulty and subjectivity of proving motive elements, such as an aim to intimidate or a political motive. Generic definitions are wider and more ambiguous than enumerative ones, although all definitions generalise, and the problem is lessened by combining generic and enumerative features in a single definition. Combined definitions are narrower than enumerative ones – since listed offences only amount to terrorism when they also satisfy a motive element – and are the most likely type of definition to satisfy the principle of legality, or specificity, in criminal offences. After 11th September, 2001, the international community is closer than ever to securing agreement on generic definition in the Sixth Committee of the General Assembly. The definition currently proposed in the Draft Comprehensive Convention has been substantially endorsed in the report of the *UN High-Level Panel on Threats, Challenges and Change in late 2004.*[113] This High-Level Panel Report also expressed its support for *the Financing Convention and Resolution 1566*, definitions by recommending that domestic legislatures refer to both definitions when drafting their own.[114]

We have discussed the general and specific approach relating to definition of terrorism. After thorough examinations of all the definitions, we can suggest three main points which will make a good definition of terrorism. These three main points are given below –

First, it is preferable to adopt a *general* approach for defining terrorism. On a practical level, this means that governments will not have to continually revisit the issue of what constitutes terrorism in order to respond to fast-developing instances of bio-terrorism, nuclear terrorism, cyber terrorism and the like. Investigative and enforcement agencies need to be able to respond quickly and with certainty to terrorist threats in the knowledge that the scenario they are faced with falls within a general category of 'terrorist acts'. This is not to say that *general* definitions of terrorism cannot benefit from *specific* elements. However, a completely *specific* approach to the problem, as has largely been adopted to date in the international legal arena, results in a piecemeal, ad hoc and reactive means of regulation. In any event, the *specific* approach lacks the wider moral-political appeal of the *general* approach, which can lead to a stronger statement about the indiscriminate use of violence to attain political, religious or ideological ends.

Secondly, a definition should make a specific exclusion at least in favour of advocacy, dissent and industrial action. While the *general* approach is preferable in that it represents a more unified and prospective approach to the legal regulation of terrorism, and makes a more compelling political statement, we must be vigilant to ensure that any description of the subject matter does not impinge unduly on democratic rights and freedoms. The breadth of the United Kingdom, United States and, especially, the Northern Territory definitions are dangerous because they may extend to acts of public protest and industrial action. Counter-terrorist legislation can be justified in the offences it creates, and the breadth of the powers that it gives to investigative and enforcement agencies, only to the extent that it actually addresses credible threats to a democratic system. It must not provide a basis for the investigation and persecution of legitimate (even if unlawful) dissent within a society.

Thirdly, Parliament should set out the core elements of any definition of terrorism. It provides the appropriate forum in which to deliberate upon the issue. Moreover, statutes have significant advantages over judicial decisions in defining such a crucial part of the law. Parliament should define the core elements of what constitutes terrorism, but in doing so must recognise that much of the work of giving meaning to these concepts will fall to the courts. This is inevitable in a common law system and represents an appropriate balance between the capacity of Parliament to set down general rules and the role of the courts in applying those rules in light of individual cases.

Actually, all these definitions mentioned above do not represent all the components of terrorism. However, if these definitions are analysed in totality, then an acceptable definition may come out. According to Wilkins the number of definitions of terrorism equals the number of works dedicated to the subject[115].

The committee of Criminal Justice Reform appointed by the Ministry of Home Affairs under the chairmanship of Dr Justice V.S. Malimath has discussed about terrorism.[116] While discussing terrorism, it admits that it is difficult to define 'terrorism,' as during the last 40 years the forms of terrorism have undergone metamorphose. However, one of the earliest definitions in the 20th Century which comes to mind, is the one given in Article 1 of the League of Nations Convention on Terrorism, 1937 which defined it as "criminal acts" directed against a State and intended or calculated to create a State of terror in the minds of particular persons, or a group of persons or the general public.[117] This definition has also undergone a change, as today terrorism is seen to be more about power – as a means to political power with full control of State authority. There has been a good deal of debate on the desirability of having a comprehensive definition as new trends and dangers have been revealed. It poses a question whether the definition should be general or enumerative or mixed or whether it should be confined to individual and group terrorism or State terrorism as well and whether it should exempt the struggles for self-determination from its scope or embrace all situations alike.[118] Accordingly, the Committee recommended that a comprehensive and inclusive definition of terrorists' acts, disruptive activities and organised crimes be provided in the Indian Penal Code 1860, so that there is no legal vacuum in dealing with terrorists, underworld criminals and their activities after special laws are permitted to lapse as in the case of TADA 1987.[119]

Bruce Hoffman while defining terrorism rightly observed the followings[120] –

> "On one point, at least, everyone agrees: terrorism is a pejorative term. It is a word with intrinsically negative connotations that is generally applied to one's enemies and opponents, or to those with whom one disagrees and would otherwise prefer to ignore. "What is called terrorism, "Brian Jenkins has written, "thus seems to depend on one's point of view. Use of the term implies a moral judgement; and if one party can successfully attach the label terrorist to its opponent, then it has indirectly persuaded others to adopt its moral viewpoint." Hence, the decision to call someone or label some organisation `terrorist' becomes almost unavoidably subjective, depending largely on whether one sympathises with or opposes the person/group/cause concerned. If one identifies with the victim of the violence, for example, then the act is terrorism. If, however, one identifies with the perpetrator, the violent act is regarded in a more sympathetic, if not positive (or, at the worst, an ambivalent) light; and it is not terrorism."

Considering all the definitions of terrorism, the main ingredients or characteristics of terrorism can be reduced as following[121] –

(i) The perpetration of violence by whatever means;

(ii) The targetting of innocent civilians;

(iii) With the intent to cause violence or with wanton disregard for its consequences;

(iv) For the purpose of causing fear, coercing or intimidating an enemy, and

(v) In order to achieve some political, military, ethnic, ideological, or religious goal.

According to the first ingredient, most times the violence associated with terrorism, which is perpetrated without any justification or excuse in an attempt to gain publicity for the cause of the terrorists. Violence can be seen in different forms and it varies depending upon the degrees of severity. However, an act is violent only if it causes harm to persons and things.[122] Violence in any form can inspire terror in its victims and in those indirectly affected by the violence. But, it is to be remembered that terrorist violence is not necessary homicidal; several non-lethal acts of violence, such as hijacking, rape, maiming, and others, are carried out by terrorists. The terms violence and terrorism are used interchangeably but they are two different concepts. It can be said that all terrorism involves violence, but not all violence is terrorism. For example, violence may be used in cases of self-defence or against legitimate targets – combatants rather than non-combatants. The definition of the terrorist act must have a link with the notion of violence and defining the latter in an appropriate way also becomes necessary. If terrorism is to be linked to violence, it is important not to use a notion of violence that is too broad. This can be appropriate in certain contexts where we may wish to talk of the violence of poverty, racism or sexism, etc. For our purposes a stricter definition of violence has to be used, namely, the exercise of force such as to physically harm, injure, pain or kill humans. Such a definition excludes damage to property and is independent of the ends or intentions or subjective perceptions of the agents of such violence.

(i) Terrorism cannot be equated with political violence, because of two reasons –

First, there are other types of political violence also, like riot, racism etc. Terrorism should be distinguished from all these forms of political violence, because identical acts performed in different situations may not be regarded as of the same kind. Actually violence means the exercise of physical force so as to inflict injury upon person or persons. But there are number of cases where physical force is not required to cause damage, such as using germs of anthrax, plague, etc. bio-chemical weapon to kill or frighten people, using radioactive material, agro-terrorism, cyber terrorism etc. For those matters violence cannot be the defining character of terrorism, though it may fairly be considered as its universally accompanying character. It seems that the factor of motivation may be considered as the defining character of terrorism, because it is motivation that makes an act what it

Secondly, because all acts of violence against governments are not acts of terrorism. For example, acts of banditry are not necessarily acts of terrorism although they may be directed against governments. Moreover, war against a governments or a revolution is surely one sort of political violence, but it cannot be categorised as terrorism.[123]

(ii) As regards the second ingredient there is no clarity as to who would actually be included in the category of innocent civilians but is more a case to case basis decision.[124] Brian Jenkins famously points out that "terrorism is theatre" and that terrorist attacks were often choreographed for the media.[125] Actually, it is more often described as an act that seeks to influence a population significantly larger than the immediate target, who are usually civilians, non-combatants, bystanders or symbolic persons and places, because the terrorists groups want to put a grievance on the public agenda, though its victims are the so-called innocent people, who generally have no role in either causing or correcting the grievance of the terrorists. The term so-called is used because the terrorists do not think of any person whatsoever (not even a child) to be innocent. It is generally believed that, the terrorists want a lot of frightened people watching rather than a lot of people dead. If anybody wants an act of violence to have the maximum psychological effect, especially in open societies where the life of ordinary people has a high value, one must target civilians. Targetting civilians are the best way to create terror and to influence the decisions of the government.

(iii) With respect to the third ingredient, most courts have established definitions of wanton disregard or intent, which is used in order to establish intent of the accused.[126] If the definition of terrorism does not include the element of intent to coerce or intimidate, then any criminal could be deemed a terrorist. Definitions of terrorism often include a description of who may be a perpetrator and who may be a target of terrorist violence (e.g., the public, the government, property). However, these definitions also attempt to set out the range of 'motives' of the perpetrator that correspond to 'terrorism', which makes 'terrorists' different from ordinary criminals. By focussing on the 'motives' and not on the 'gravity' of the act, definitions of terrorism becomes overly broad. The motive of the offender must be distinguished from the intent. Regarding terrorism, the motive will be to attain a political goal (such as to alter or destroy the fundamental principles and pillars of a country or international organisation). The intent will be to intimidate a population or part of it. Some states, such as the Russian Federation and the People's Republic of China, think that every act of violence carried out by irregular fighters against the state must be called 'terrorist.' Other states consider every act of violence against civilians or non-combatants a terrorist act, even if it is carried out by a state or by an official institution.[127] So, these two definitions are not same and they are incompatible, in the first case, terrorism is the enemy of the state; in the second case, it is the enemy of the society.

(iv) The fourth ingredient is the purpose of causing fear, coercing or intimidating an enemy. Actually, one of the objects of terrorism is to produce fear. The purpose, direction, and focus of terrorism are fear. Terrorists attempt, by the nature of indiscriminate acts of violence, to manipulate fear to achieve a variety of tactical and political objections. This fear is generally produced to the civilians not to the soldiers or policemen. Killing the soldiers or policemen does not frighten the others and obviously their reaction will be to urge their officers to lead them out with their guns to find the killer. On the other hand, if a member of a family is killed by terrorists on the street outside his home, everyone on that street will be in terror as it may happen to them also. Terrorists wanted maximum publicity for their acts, playing for an audience and spreading their ideological message. This dramatic and shocking incidents of violence would attrack attention of the people. The atmosphere of fear so created by terrorism, often influence people to exaggerate the importance of the cause of terrorism and strengthen the force and also movement of terrorism. Terrorist attack are often carefully choreographed to attract the attention of the electronic media and the international press. Individual act of terrorism also may be aimed at extracting specific concessions, such as payment of ransom, the release of prisoners or publication of terrorist message. Terrorists often seek to improve their bargaining power by creating a dramatic hostage situation that might coerce a government into meeting their demands. Actually, terrorism is not measured by body counts or property damaged, but rather by its psychological effects and its political results. It is true that terrorism pursues its aim by creating a situation of fear (and more precisely of terror) in a group or in a population. This is why; terrorism is widely seen as an extreme form of violence. However, terrorism is considered an extreme form of violence because it has a psychological impact much deeper than its physical consequences.

(v) The final and most important ingredient of terrorism is a purpose or goal, which can be one of many such as a political, military, ethnic, ideological, or religious cause. The overriding purpose is a necessary element of the definition.[128] The final ingredient of terrorism, that is with respect to a motive or goal is of particular importance in a definition of terrorism in the Indian scenario.

(vi) *First*, it attempts to take away from all groups the right to legitimise violence as a part of a larger social movement.[129] Furthermore, it lends more clarity to the definition and helps differentiate terrorism from other crimes. This common denominator found in most definitions of terrorism is the achievement of some vague political objective. The political content of the act of terrorism distinguishes it from such ordinary criminal activities as murder, robbery, kidnapping, extortion, and hijacking, all of which are committed with far greater frequency by 'non-terrorists' for motives of simple profit or passion. However, it is obvious that terror and terrorism need not be always politically motivated. For example, first, criminals frequently resort to terrorist-type tactics for personal gain. Fleeing felons, upon encountering the police, will often take hostages and attempt to negotiate their escape. *Secondly*, mentally disturbed persons may also terrorise others because of their condition.

(vii) *Thirdly*, some individuals may terrorise others because they are bored, sadistic, or angry, which causes them to engage in some type of violent act of protest against society.

Each of these understandings carries grave problems. Intimidation is too loose and broad a concept. There are many kinds or forms of organised intimidation including systems or structures of psychological intimidation at various degrees and levels. Terrorism needs not only have civilian and non-combatants as targets. Terrorist acts can also be inflicted on combatants as well. When indefensible violence or extreme disproportion in violence is used against opposing combatants, such as the use of nuclear or chemical or biological warfare, this too can count as terrorism. One does not have to go so far as to use weapons of mass destruction. Simply using tanks or bombers to destroy a militant hideout where the defenders are known to only have rifles can also count as an indefensible terrorist act. The US Military considers the attacks on military installations or on armed military personnel when a state of military hostilities does not exist at the site, such as bombing against US bases, etc., as acts of terrorism. As for terrorism being the indiscriminate use of violence, so much of what we understand as terrorist acts or events involve very specific, indeed highly discriminate use of violence.

Finally, assigning the label of terrorism to only those acts deemed illegitimate begs all questions about the legitimacy of the 'officially' legitimate wielders of violence – the state. Such an approach is far too narrow, for it definitionally outlaws even the possibility of state terrorism.

If terrorism is defined strictly in terms of attacks of non-military targets, a number of attacks on military installations and soldiers' residences could not be included in the statistics. In order to cut through the Gordian definitional knot, terrorism expert A. Schmid suggested in 1992 in a report for the then UN Crime Branch that it might be a good idea to take the existing consensus on what constitutes a 'war crime' as a point of departure. If the core of war crimes – deliberate attacks on civilians, hostage taking and the killing of prisoners – is extended to peacetime, we could simply define acts of terrorism as 'peacetime equivalents of war crimes.[130]

However, the above characteristics or ingredients have faced criticism on the following grounds:

(i) *Firstly*, the political nature of terrorism is also challenged by several scholars, according to them, in the present day international mass terrorism has no political goal as it does not plan to build a new social or political order. Its only aim is the destruction of the political sphere itself.

(ii) *Secondly,* the psychological side of terrorism is also questioned. In the past and as well as today several forms of terrorism are not meant to create a situation of fear. Even some try to provoke anger or revenge. In other respects, because of the possibility that terrorists use weapons of mass destruction, it is not legitimate anymore to claim that terrorist attacks are solely psychological.

(iii) *Finally,* one can criticise the victim-based definition of terrorism. The victims of terrorism are not necessarily civilians and they are not always targetted at random. Of course, certain terrorist groups expressly deny the distinction between combatants and non-combatants. But certain other groups respect the distinction.

As per *Report by Lord Carlile of Berriew Q.C*, presented to Parliament by the Secretary of State for the Home Department, United

Kingdom[131] there are several broad propositions as to what should not be included in such a definition. These are as follows:

(i) Offences against property should not be included in a definition of terrorism;

(ii) Offences for a religious purpose should be excluded, as religion is a diffuse concept incapable of clear definition;

(iii) There should be exclusion of offences akin to terrorism, but not really terrorist is anything more than means of perpetration, i.e., lacking a sufficient political or ideological component/motive;

(iv) Mere preaching or glorification should not be capable of being regarded as terrorist offences;

(v) Terrorism in a just cause, on the basis that what is terrorism against an oppressive regime may be justifiable if to assist freedom fighters;

Without a definition of terrorism, one could neither identify an act of violence as terrorist nor condemn nor justify that act. When one tries to define terrorism, one is, in the first place, astonished by the multiplicity of definitions already proposed by different philosophers, experts and scholars. They are so different that no consensus seems likely to be reached. The UN Security Council in its 2002 report of the *UN Policy Working Group on the UN and Terrorism* pointed out some guidance and principles in this regard[132]–

> "Without attempting a comprehensive definition of terrorism, it would be useful to delineate some broad characteristics of the phenomenon. Terrorism is, in most cases, essentially a political act. It is meant to inflict dramatic and deadly injury on civilians and to create an atmosphere of fear, generally for a political or ideological (whether secular or religious) purpose. Terrorism is a criminal act, but it is more than mere criminality. To overcome the problem of terrorism it is necessary to understand its political nature as well as its basic criminality and psychology".

In late 2004, the Secretary-General of the United Nations presented the report of the High-level Panel on Threats, Challenges and Change to the General Assembly, which was compiled by a panel of experts appointed by the Secretary-General.[133] In this report, UN experts pointed out that, despite the debates of numerous workgroups throughout several decades, the member states did not manage to reach any consensus concerning the definition of terrorism.[134]

According to this Report,

"The definition of terrorism should include the following elements[135] –

(a) Recognition, in the preamble, that State use of force against civilians is regulated by the Geneva Conventions and other instruments, and, of sufficient scale, constitutes a war crime by the persons concerned or a crime against humanity;

(b) Restatement that acts under the 12 preceding anti-terrorism conventions are terrorism, and a declaration that they are a crime under international law; and restatement that terrorism in time of armed conflict is prohibited by the Geneva Conventions and Protocols;

(c) Reference to the definitions contained in the 1999 International Convention for the Suppression of the Financing of Terrorism and Security Council Resolution 1566 (2004);

(d) Description of terrorism as "any action, in addition to actions already specified by the existing conventions on aspects of terrorism, the Geneva Conventions and Security Council Resolution 1566 (2004), that is intended to cause death or serious bodily harm to civilians or non-combatants, when the purpose of such an act, by its nature or context, is to intimidate a population, or to compel a Government or an international organisation to do or to abstain from doing any act".

Furthermore, the recent and most promising attempts to formulate a definition of terrorism completely failed. In 2005, neither the UN Summit[136] nor the Euromed Summit[137] adopted a definition of terrorism. Even though the final declarations of these summits emphasised the necessity of such a definition, none of them provided the slightest definitional element of terrorism. The summits firmly condemned terrorism without defining it.

Martin Scheinin, the United Nations special rapporteur on the promotion and protection of human rights and fundamental freedoms while countering terrorism, has highlighted the risks of codifying vague and overly broad definitions of terrorism and related terms into law.[138] He further observed that the international framework on counter-terrorism, through the principal anti-terrorism conventions, and resolutions of the Security Council, General Assembly and Commission on Human Rights impose obligations and issue instructions to States on the question of terrorism without there being a comprehensive definition of the term. This is not only problematic for States in their ability to determine levels of proper compliance with those conventions and resolutions, but it also bears upon other matters. Different elements within the domestic terrorism offences of separate States are likely to pose difficulties for both extradition and mutual legal assistance.[139]

Terrorism is, no doubt, a particular form of violence. But still it differs from other forms of violence, which endanger our existence, such as war, revolution, guerrilla warfare, insurgency, communal riots, ordinary crime etc. First of all, we have to distinguish terrorism from the above forms of violence to define terrorism. Unless and until we know the difference it will be hard to distinguish it from the above forms of violence.

Crime and Terrorism

Terrorism was condemned by the General Assembly as criminal because it was believed that there may be a chance of mitigating international terrorism if the states consider terrorism as a crime under international law. Even in the *League of Nations Convention on terrorism, 1937*, terrorism was referred as criminal acts directed against a state and intended or calculated to create a state of terror in the minds of particular persons or a group of persons or the general public. Crime is explained in the *Dictionary of Behavioural Science* as 'major transgression of the law, which is punishable'.[140] According to *Black's Law Dictionary*[141] 'crime means an act that the law makes punishable.' There are various forms of crime but the core essence of all those forms is deviation from behaviour sanctioned by the criminal law – such behaviour is punishable under the penal code.

To identify whether terrorism is a crime or not, a first step is to look at what crime is. It is impossible to give a universal description or definition of 'what crime is'. In the normal context, the influences on what people or society considers being a crime are large in number, varying from media influence and religious beliefs to the factor of time. Thus, in contemporary criminological literature, the conceptualisation of an act as a crime is seen as dependant on the context of the act, the outcome of it and the individual or group defining it. This defining is mostly done by codifying certain behaviour or acts, and of course their outcomes, into laws. To clarify the subjective scope of the construct of crime, an example will be used: rape in marriage. Raping one's wife was not acknowledged as a criminal act for a long time. Even in contemporary times, it does not constitute a crime in some countries, and in many, it is (still) not punishable.

Other examples include adultery and homosexuality, which are still harshly prosecuted in some countries and can even result in the death penalty. In other countries, homosexuality and adultery are seen as normal and have not been criminalised at all.

Thus, there are basically two different vantage points of conceptualising crime. The first is that every forbidden act or result of an act can be categorised as a crime. The definitions of this narrow concept of crime vary widely. *The Encyclopaedia Britannica*,[142] for example, states the following definition: 'intentional commission of an act usually deemed socially harmful or dangerous and specifically defined, prohibited and punishable under the criminal law'. This is an even narrower concept of crime; it includes only acts which are codified as wrong in criminal law (written laws) and not in common law (civil law), like, for example, the law related to treaties or private law. The second way of conceptualising crime takes a broader approach and involves looking at socially (un) acceptable conduct. This includes acts codified in laws and, on the other end of the scope, also forbidden acts that are hardly ever punished anymore because of the influence of public opinion. In most countries, there is a good example of a codified crime which is accepted as non-criminal by such a large part of society that it generally is not punished as severely as was the case previously, such as public drunkenness, for example. This second approach to crime leaves even more room for debate than the first and it is deemed unsuitable by most criminologists for studying and examining crime in an effective way.

Nevertheless, it should be pointed out that this approach is a more valid way of reconstructing what crime is because it takes in all aspects of construction, as opposed to the narrow approach. The above-mentioned complexity also applies to terrorism, and the question arises whether terrorism is a form of crime or not. When it comes to terrorist acts, a narrow definition of terrorism that focusses on the mala *per se* crimes is desirable, since there is widespread international consensus on this type of crime. Terrorism can be seen as a broad concept including a variety of acts such as carrying out bombings etc.[143]

In every criminal offence comprise the elements of *mens rea* (criminal consciousness) and *actus reus* (the description of the criminal act). The description of the *actus reus* should, in the case of terrorism, make clear in what sense the offence is different from other criminal acts, such as, for example, murder or assault. When comparing the different definitions, it becomes clear that all fulfill the definitional element with regard to the *mens rea* aspect. Most definitions use words as intent, intentionally or willfully. One definition refers to a criminal plan that has to lie on the basis of the actions, which also suggests that there was a prior intention to commit a certain act. With regard to the definitional element of 'purpose' clearly most definitions use terms like 'intimidating the population' 'provoking a state of terror', or 'compelling a government or an international organisation in doing or abstaining from doing an act'.

The acts of crime having distinctive features differ from terrorism.

(i) *First,* the acts of terrorism are executed with the deliberate intention of causing panic, disorder and terror within an organised society; in order to destroy social discipline, paralyse the forces of reaction of a society and to increase the misery and suffering of the community. This intentional element is one of the major points of distinction between crime and terrorism. An act of terrorism must involve the intention to create or cause civil instability. Even crimes like mass murder are not to be identified with terrorism because they lack that particular intention.

(ii) *Secondly,* a criminal is branded as terrorist when he indulges in criminal acts with an illegitimate political motive irrespective of the fact whether his targets and victims were international or otherwise. An ordinary criminal, on the other hand, is a person who commits a criminal act with "required criminal intent" irrespective of motive. Therefore, mainly it is the political motive, which distinguishes a terrorist from an ordinary criminal.

(iii) *Thirdly,* while common criminals usually try to avoid detection, terrorists often seek attention and exposure. As it is already discussed that terrorists want maximum publicity for their actions. Terrorists are looking for exposure and have, in regard to their actions, a symbiotic relationship with the media and governmental impact, unlike organised crime.

(iv) *Fourthly,* terrorist acts are planned and executed, almost always, by an organisation however small it may be, but never by any sole individual independently. Terrorism requires an organisation, and in such an organisation the members act under the belief that their actions are acts of war against an illegitimate government. Generally, the acts of violence perpetrated by terrorists are ideologically motivated. This is not true in case of crime.

(v) *Fifthly,* crime is defined by the criminal law of a nation or state or local jurisdiction where it is being committed but terrorism is not defined by any such criminal law.

(vi) *Sixthly,* crime generally committed for personal gain but terrorism has a different goal altogether and hence it differs from crime. No terrorist ever commits an act of violence for personal gain.

(vii) *Seventhly,* crime has never been, or can never be characterised by struggle for freedom, which is often ascribed to terrorism. That is the reason for saying that – 'one man's terrorist is another man's freedom fighter.'

Though sometimes terrorism is described as 'international crime' but at best it can be termed as 'political crime' and it can never be generalised as 'violent crime.' Terrorist methods have undoubtedly been used as useful weapons by the revolutionaries, by the insurgents and by the guerrillas all over the world. But we should not hesitate to differentiate terrorism from all the other forms of violence. Guns are always used in a battle as weapons but they are not identical. Terrorism does surely have a political motivation, and thus must not be considered as ordinary or common crime in any way. Terroristic motivation may not necessarily include political goal as Schmid has pointed out in his definition, it may be criminal in nature or may be an act of vengeance or even religious or social in nature.

Terrorism and War

War is an act of violence intended to compel our opponent to fulfill our will. According to *Black's Law Dictionary,*[144] war means 'hostile conflict by means of armed forces, carried on between nations, states or rules or sometimes between parties within the same nation or state.' *Chambers 21st Century Dictionary*[145] defines war as 'an open state of armed conflict, especially between nations.' Though terrorism has similar operational conditions like war, but two operations differ in their characters. The nature and characteristics of terrorism reveals that terrorism differs from war. Some facts are given below:

(i) Terrorism does not take place between political units. Terrorism can be practiced by the state against its citizens or by certain political or religious groups against the system of governance or even one particular community against some other community within the state territory. But war should take place between political units.

(ii) The hostility created by terrorism does not necessarily need to reach a certain magnitude, nor does it need to continue actively for certain duration. In case of war inflicted violence should reach a certain magnitude and it should go on for a certain duration.

(iii) Terrorism initiates fear psychosis. The actual or the threatened fear is created, unlike war, among the non-combatants to fulfil the purpose of the terrorists.

(iv) The concept of two contending groups is nonexistent in case of terrorism; it is mostly a one way attitude where the victims are innocent. So equality of authority and power is not relevant. In war the contending groups should be equal in power.

(v) Terrorism in some cases is a state instrument only, but there are other forms of terrorism also where it is not a state instrument. War is a state instrument by which one state can compel its opponent to fulfil its will.

(vi) Terrorism as a means to achieve political goal, does not emerge due to any threat to the very survival of the state, because in most of the cases the state or the government itself is the target of the terrorists. War involves armed conflict – specially the military instrument of the state.

(vii) Terrorism does not usually involve two state forces and hence the question of exercising free will of the victim does not arise at all. War involves at least two state forces each of which is free to exercise its independent will.

(viii) Terrorism has no legitimate and internationally recognised strategy or tactic. It improvises its own means, methods and tactics to suit its own purpose and motive. These usually differ from one group to another. They recognise no non-combatants, no bystanders. Innocence is irrelevant to their lexicon, and even women and children are made victims to intensify their perpetrated threat and fear. But in case of war it must have a legitimate strategy and a legitimate tactic, which is internationally recognised (it has rules to conform to and conventions to follow, which grant immunity from deliberate attack on civilian non-combatants and it recognises neutral territory).

(ix) The question of state sovereignty being attacked by some foreign force is totally irrelevant in case of terrorism. War involves an attack on sovereignty.

(x) The centre of power and authority in case of terrorism is definable in some cases but in no case is it constitutional and formal. In case of interstate of war the locus of authority and power is clearly definable, which is the constitutional system of governance of the states.

(xi) The rules of war grant civilian non-combatants at least theoretical immunity from deliberate attack, prohibit taking civilian hostages, prohibit actions against those held captive and they recognise neutral territory, but terrorist recognise no neutral territory and they seize and often murder hostages.

(xii) The limitations declared by the rules of war do not apply in case of terrorism, because terrorism does not have any such limitations but rules of war declare certain limitations.

Terrorism and Guerrilla Warfare

Terrorism and guerrilla warfare often serves as alternative designations of the same phenomenon. Most often terrorism is identified with guerrilla warfare because of some of their apparent methodical similarities. Actually they are not only unidentical but they are distinctly different. Guerrilla warfare is a form of warfare by which the strategically weaker side fights against the state force. According to Mao Zedong guerrillas are 'fishes' that swim in the waters of the society. According to *Black's Law Dictionary*[146] Guerrilla warfare means 'hostilities that are conducted by individuals or small groups who are usually not part of an organised army and who fight by means of surprise attacks, ambushes and sabotage. Formerly, it was thought that the hostilities had to be conducted in enemy occupied territory. Typically, guerrilla warfare is carried out only when geographical conditions are favourable and when the civilian population is at least partly cooperative.' According to *Chambers 21st Century Dictionary,*[147] Guerrilla warfare means 'a member of a small, independent, often politically motivated armed force making surprise attacks, e.g., against government troops.' The main difference between those two are given below:

(i) One of the defining characters of guerrilla warfare is people's sympathy, co-operation and assistance. Mao Zedong believed that without a political goal guerrilla warfare must fail, as it must if its political objectives do not coincide with the aspirations of the people and their sympathy, co-operation and assistance cannot be gained. Assistance and support mean support by furnishing money, food, shelter, refuge, transport, medical aid, intelligence and even by furnishing their sons and daughters as recruits. But terrorism has no such unreserved support of the majority of the country' populace and hence is called low-level violence, which lacks significant popular support.

(ii) Terrorism is always practiced by a segment of the society, where the majority of the nation's interest is not the agenda and though terror is a consequence of the main weapons used in guerrilla warfare not all guerrilla leaders have favoured the use of terrorist tactics; whereas in case of terrorism creating terror, actual or symbolic, is the only method. The presence of violence is a fundamental characteristic of terrorism and with it is added criminality.

(iii) Almost all forms of terrorist activities involve criminal acts such as murder, assault, hijacking, kidnapping, sabotage etc., which are subject to be dealt under international criminal law. But guerrilla warfare does not involve criminality in the way terrorism does.

(iv) Guerrilla warfare is always conducted within the territorial jurisdiction of the state, i.e., the perpetration of violence does not cross its territory. But terrorism has an inherent tendency to cross the border, where it becomes international in nature.

(v) Though guerrilla warfare is conducted by unconventional means, it is carried out with real military aims and targets. But terrorism is not necessarily targetted against regular military forces. It is planned for public effect, not for military objectives.

(vi) In case of terrorism, it mostly target their attacks on innocent non-combatants, who are not even remotely concerned with their goal or who have no direct connection with the causes to which the terrorists are dedicated. But in case of guerrilla warfare, it accepts the principal convention of war which never targets innocent people.

(vii) Guerrilla respects the rights of non-combatants, but terrorists place no limits on the means employed and frequently do they resort to harming civilian population. So intending targets of attack is the main factor. If an attack deliberately targets civilians or non-combatants, then it will be considered to be a terrorist attack, whereas if it targets regular military forces, then it will be considered a guerrilla attack.

Terrorism and Insurgency

According to the *International Encyclopaedia of Government and Politics*, insurgency is an extra-legal means of altering political systems, usually with the goal of changing the leadership.[148] According to *Black's Law Dictionary*,[149] *Insurgent* means 'a person who, for political purposes, engages in armed hostility against an established government.' According to Chambers 21st Century Dictionary[150] Insurgent mean 'an uprising or rebellion.' According to T.E. Arnold, the main ingredients of insurgency are[151] –

(i) Fighting against foreign domination and alien occupation and against repressive regimes to over through such power;

(ii) They do this in the exercise of their right to self-determination.

The main differences between the two are given below:

(i) The goal of insurgency is overt throwing the existing government or political leadership due to lack of transparency in the legitimacy of the ruling authorities or their policies. Insurgency takes resort to various means, of which guerrilla warfare is one, though resorting to unconventional warfare and terroristic methods is not rare. The nature of insurgency as a negative force, though unlawful but it is not criminal. Hence, it is a form of violence distinctly different from terrorism. According to Arnold, terrorism is usually placed in the category of violent crimes against people, which should be dealt with severely under the penal code, while insurgency is placed in a class of small-scale military or paramilitary activity that should be dealt with under the international rules of armed conflict.[152]

(ii) The objective of the insurgents differs from that of the terrorists. Insurgency never involves non-combatant victims, because, primarily, it is a method of war. On the other hand, terrorists do not have any purely military mission, so their victims are arbitrarily chosen in order to propagate fear more widely.

Terrorism never intends to alter or change a government or regime. It has a political goal where the indiscriminate means of violence are intertwined. This differs from that of insurgency, which has. In addition, a positive socio-cultural and political goal of asserting the right of self-determination. The positive goal of self-determination, which kindles the fire in the people collectively, insults insurgency from terrorism. Terrorism, in various cases, aims at vengeance. So mere use of terrorist tactics (like kidnapping, assassination, hijacking, etc.) cannot identify insurgency with terrorism.

Whether Terrorism is an Act of War or a Criminal Act

Now, the crucial question for determination is whether we should consider terrorism as an act of war or a criminal act. Already we have distinguished terrorism from war on several grounds.

Since 1979, there is still a lack of a clear and acceptable definition of terrorism, the General Assembly made the distinction that terrorism is a crime which should be prosecuted within the legal system, rather than viewing terrorism as an act of war. In *Resolution 34/145*,[153] the General Assembly called upon states to work together in order to prevent and combat terrorism through the exchange of information, and creation of treaties allowing for the 'extradition and prosecution of international terrorists.' This provision was included again in *Resolution 38/130*,[154] *Resolution 40/61*,[155] *Resolution 42/159*[156] and *Resolution 44/29*.[157] In 1991, the General Assembly recognised all of the above provisions and determined that the issue of terrorism should be included in its provisional agenda under the shortened title 'Measures to Eliminate International Terrorism.'[158]

In 1995, the General Assembly appeared to take a more direct stance that terrorism is a crime, not an act of war, by approving the Declaration on Measures to Eliminate International Terrorism, attached in the annex of the Resolution 49/60.[159] In the Preamble, this Declaration listed terrorism as a crime closely connected to crimes such as 'drug-trafficking, unlawful arms trade, money laundering and smuggling of nuclear and other potentially deadly materials' etc., and reiterated that those responsible for acts of terrorism 'must be brought to justice.'

Additionally, in the Declaration, the General Assembly appears to have created a definition of terrorism, which stated "criminal acts intended or calculated to provoke a state of terror in the general public, a group of persons or particular persons for political purposes are in any circumstance unjustifiable, whatever the considerations of a political, philosophical, ideological, racial, ethnic, religious or any other nature that may be invoked to justify them."[160] This Declaration clearly views terrorism as a criminal act, rather than an act of war. This "definition" was cited throughout the subsequent resolutions issued up until September 11, 2001, such as in Resolution 55/158,[161] Resolution 54/110,[162] Resolution 53/108,[163] Resolution 52/165,[164] Resolution 51/210[165] and Resolution 50/53.[166]

After the terrorist attacks on September 11, 2001, the General Assembly in its Resolution 56/1[167] condemned the terrorist attacks on the United States and called for those responsible to be "brought to justice." The wording of this Resolution indicates that the General Assembly continued to view terrorism as a 'crime' rather than an act of war. By January 2002, the General Assembly reiterated the 'definition' that terrorism is a crime, as set forth in the Declaration on Measures to Eliminate International Terrorism, such as Resolution 46/51,[168] Resolution 49/60[169] and Resolution 56/88[170]. Resolution 56/88 also stressed the need for states to become parties to those conventions and protocols that address terrorism, and to enact the legislation 'necessary to implement the provisions of those conventions and protocols, to ensure that the jurisdiction of their courts enables them to bring to trial the perpetrators of terrorist acts.'[171] The provisions in Resolution 56/88 relating to terrorism as a crime have continued to be adhered to and reiterated in the subsequent 'Measures to Eliminate International Terrorism' Resolutions issued by the General Assembly afterwards, such as Resolution 57/27[172], Resolution 58/81[173] and Resolution59/46[174]. So, it is crystal clear that the General Assembly has, with its series of resolutions, determined that terrorism is a crime, not an act of war.

The Security Council has taken the position that terrorism is a crime rather than an act of war. Immediately after 9/11 the Security Council issued Resolution 1368 in which it condemned the terrorist attacks in New York, and called upon all States to 'work together urgently to bring to justice the perpetrators, organisers and sponsors of these terrorist attacks and stressed that those responsible for aiding, supporting or harbouring the perpetrators, organisers, and sponsors of these acts will be held accountable.'[175] Here, the Security Council likewise could have defined terrorism as an act of war; however, they carefully crafted their words to define terrorism as a crime for which the perpetrators of such acts must be brought to justice.

Although the Security Council members defined terrorism as a crime immediately after 9/11, its approach did not remain consistent, and a mixed response followed only sixteen days later.[176] In the Preamble of its Resolution 1373, the Security Council contradicted its earlier statement that terrorism is a crime, when it reaffirmed the right to individual or collective self-defence under the UN Charter, and reaffirmed the 'need to combat terrorist acts by all means' in accordance with the UN Charter. Later, in the same Resolution, the Security Council required that terrorist acts be established as 'serious criminal offences in domestic laws and regulations and that the punishment duly reflects the seriousness of such terrorist acts.' This mixed response was a result of the lack of a clear and acceptable definition of terrorism.

Since Resolution 1373, the Security Council has returned to its original definition of terrorism as a crime, rather than an act of war. In further Resolutions, issued by the Security Council from 2001 to 2012, the Security Council has continued to maintain that terrorism is a crime, such as Resolution 1377,[177] Resolution 1456,[178] Resolution 1566,[179] Resolution 1636,[180] Resolution 1644,[181] Resolution 1664,[182] Resolution 1735,[183] Resolution 1757,[184] Resolution 1822,[185] Resolution 1852,[186] Resolution 1904,[187] Resolution 1963,[188] Resolution 1989[189] and Resolution 2083.[190]

The use of terror or violence in itself does not constitute terrorism because terror may be used for criminal or personal ends. Conceptually, public order and terrorism are different not only in ideology and philosophy but also in terms of mens rea the manner of its commission and the effect or result of such activity. Public order is well-understood and comprehended as problem associated with law and order. Terrorism is a new crime far serious in nature, more grave in impact, and highly dangerous in consequence. Terrorism may be political in nature coupled with unjustifiable use of force, threatening security and integrity of the state.

In the case of terrorism the activity which is sought to be punished has to be such which cannot be classified as a mere law and order problem or as disturbance of public order. Terrorism cannot be tackled as an ordinary criminal activity under the ordinary penal law by the normal law.

The definition of terrorism must not be too narrow nor too broad. The impropriety of the definition of terrorism has serious consequences not only from an epistemological but also from an ethical and political point of view. If one makes a too narrow definition, one can easily be suspected of partiality. Furthermore, if one makes a broad definition of terrorism, one tends to support the idea that all acts of political violence are equally legitimate. The idea that terrorism is a political violence based on the use of terror is not accepted proposition sometime. This definition does not deny the existence of a state terrorism and also terrorism in warfare.[191]

There are several types of violence that are not considered terrorist, such as nuclear deterrence, certain police operations, and mass rapes etc. The terror-based definition is therefore too broad.

In a report to the UN Human Rights Council, Scheinin, Special Rapporteur on Counter-Terrorism, argued that it is important for states to abide by the principle of legality because imprecise and overbroad definitions of terrorism give governments the opportunity to target sections of the community with no real connection to terrorism.[192]

Typologies of Terrorism

The first condition of a proper definition of terrorism is to take into account the diversity of terrorism. Terrorism is not a monolithic phenomenon; there are different types of terrorism. Now, due to this typology, we can recognise the diversity of terrorism without giving up the idea of a definition. In order to produce such a typology, we must pay attention to the multiple descriptions of the innumerable terrorist groups. Moreover, a typology favours a descriptive approach to terrorism. A typology is a categorisation of phenomena or objects in order to make them more manageable for analysis. Typologies are useful tools for researchers to frame many facets of, for example, terrorism into a single word or (the other way around) to deconstruct a phenomenon in order to find the multiple facets.

According to *Oxford Advanced Learner's Dictionary,* 'typology means' a system of dividing things into different types.[193] The guidelines used to make these categorisations or classifications can range from self-defined to theoretical considerations. This entails that the functionality of a typology is mostly defined by the purpose of the user: different objectives make for different typologies.[194] The user making the typology is an important consideration, which has a profound effect on the number of terrorism typologies in use in academic literature. There is still lack of consensus on the nature of terrorism, which relates to the quests for definition and its precise content (classification of types). As Laqueur rightly points out that any attempt to define terrorism is bound to fail, for the simple reason that there is not one but many terrorisms.[195] But the reason for the plural character of conclusions is not identical. Yet, it may also lie in the nature of the situation in which different definitions are sought for different purposes.

The first condition of a proper definition of terrorism is to take into account the different types of terrorism. Terrorism is not a monolithic phenomenon. One could object that such a statement supports the position of those, who reject the possibility of a definition. But by this, we can recognise the diversity of terrorism without giving up the idea of a definition. In order to produce such a typology, we must pay attention to the multiple descriptions of the innumerable terrorist groups. Yet, we are also bound to make an effort at generalisation. A typology could be a good compromise between the abstraction of a general definition and the confusion of particular descriptions. With this typology, every type of terrorism could be judged according to its peculiar characteristics. A typology is a classification system, and there are as many typologies of terrorism as there are definitions. Although, the introduction of a typology does not put an end to the debate about the nature of terrorism, but it does draw the limits of the discussion. Typologies are not a panacea, and they do not solve all the definitional dilemmas. The process of terrorism is in a constant state of change. Models, taxonomies, and typologies only describe patterns among events. They are generalisations that describe extremely unstable environments. Typologies may increase our understanding of terrorism, but each terrorist incident must be understood in its specific social, historical, and political circumstances. In order to build a typology, the pertinent principles of classification may be as follows:

First of them is the quantity and the status of the victims and the targets. Several cases can be distinguished. Terrorist attacks can target persons and/or material goods. And, among persons, they can target non-combatants and/or combatants. That well-known dichotomy is fundamental for the *jus in bello,* but is not sufficient; there is a whole continuum of targets and victims. The quantity of victims must also be taken into account. It does not mean that the murder of two men is more condemnable than the murder of only one, but the nature of terrorism varies also with the quantity of victims. One could object that increasing the number of victims derives only from the traditional conception of terrorism; it is meant to attract the attention of the public, albeit one much too used to bombings and killings. But mass murder can also be the sign that maybe bombings are now goals in themselves and not messages. Consequently, we have to reconsider the idea that terrorism is intrinsically an indirect strategy where the victims are distinct from the targets.

The *second* parameter of the typology is the terrorist's *modus operandi*. That trait is often seen as unimportant. On the contrary, it is quite crucial. The means chosen by the terrorists reflect the nature of their activity. One must of course take into account the type of weapons used by terrorists. The terrorists who use weapons of mass destruction (poison gas, 'dirty bombs,' biological weapons, etc.) are distinct from the ones, who use weapons the effect of which they can completely control (handguns, knives, etc.). These two types of terrorists do not have the same conception of the acts they carry out. In the first case, violence is largely indiscriminate. In the second one, it is (or at least may be) highly selective. The choice of a *modus operandi* is not determined by circumstances or by technological constraints; it is deeply rooted in the conception terrorists have of their own activity. A hijacking has not the same signification as a bomb attack. For example, hijacking is often used by what many specialists call 'advertising terrorism'; it is done primarily to draw the attention of the public on a problem, not to spread terror.

The *third* principle of the typology is focussed on what one may call 'terrorist effects.' In many cases, the main effect is terror. But these are not the only effects terrorism produces. The most important difference may be between on one hand, terrorists, who favour the intensity of the psychological shock to the detriment of the clarity of the message and on the other hand, the terrorists, who favour the content of their message and the precision of their result.

The *fourth* and last major parameter of the typology on terrorism is the goals. Some scholars claim that one should not take that parameter into account unless one wants to adopt the terrorists' point of view. According to them, the description of these goals is always binary because terrorists distinguish their cause as just and other causes as unjust. Indeed, every terrorist thinks his cause is just. Certain forms of terrorism have institutional goals; they may, for instance, want to promote a new regime. But some other forms have indeterminate and vague goals or no goal at all.

There are numbers of typologies around on terrorism typologies. One of the first systematic studies undertaken to catalogue all typologies of terrorism in order to make a general definition of terrorism is Schmid and Jongman's 1988 landmark study.[196] According to them, there are ten bases for classification:

(i) Actor-based, (ii) Victim-based,
(iii) Cause-based, (iv) Environment-based,
(v) Means-based, (vi) Political-orientation-based,
(vii) Motivation-based, (viii) Purpose-based,
(ix) Demand-based, and (x) Target-based.

Schmid and Jongman examine three of these classifications more closely. The first is the actor-based typology, which is one of the most obvious divisions – terrorism is perpetrated by an actor or actors- and thus typologies to be made for terrorism. Perpetrators of terrorism range from lone-wolf terrorists to states of governments using terrorist tactics. A second typology that Schmid and Jongman recognise is the political orientation-based one. This typology goes beyond the question of the actors involved and classifies the motivational base or origin of the organisation. The third typology Schmid and Jongman analyse is the purpose-based typology. The overlying purpose of terrorism is to terrorise a group or state. Next to these three bases for creating classifications and thus typologies, Schmid and Jongman also address the purpose and existence of multi-dimensional typologies. These typologies classify terrorism according to more than one of the above mentioned natures, or bases. One can clearly see that the nature of the goals the terrorists are aiming at must be taken into account. It does not justify terrorism. It is a key parameter to understanding the differences in terrorism, and therefore a key parameter to a typological definition of terrorism.

The use of terror or violence in itself does not constitute terrorism because terror may be used for criminal or personal ends. Conceptually, public order and terrorism are different not only in ideology and philosophy but also in terms of *mens rea* the manner of its commission and the effect or result of such activity. Public order is well-understood and comprehended as problem associated with law and order. Terrorism is a new crime far serious in nature, more grave in impact, and highly dangerous in consequence. Terrorism may be political in nature coupled with unjustifiable use of force, threatening security and integrity of the state.

In the case of terrorism, the activity which is sought to be punished has to be such which cannot be classified as a mere law and order problem or as disturbance of public order. Terrorism cannot be tackled as an ordinary criminal activity under the ordinary penal law by the normal law enforcement agencies. The cause and the intended act and reach of the criminal activity of the terrorist is such that they transcend the gravity of mere disturbance of public order and may at times the frontiers of the country. This may include such anti-national activity which throws a challenge to the integrity and sovereignty of the country. For example, if a person goes on a shooting spree and kills a number of persons, he is bound to create terror and panic in the locality but it is not a terrorist act.[197] Unless and until, it satisfies the other requirements of terrorist acts it will not constitute a terrorist act under the domestic law.

The definition of terrorism must not be too narrow nor too broad. The impropriety of the definition of terrorism has serious consequences not only from an epistemological but also from an ethical and political point of view. If one makes a too narrow definition, one can easily be suspected of partiality. Furthermore, if one makes a broad definition of terrorism, one tends to support the idea that all acts of political violence are equally legitimate. The idea that terrorism is a political violence based on the use of terror is not accepted proposition sometime.

This definition does not deny the existence of a state terrorism and also terrorism in warfare. There are several types of violence that are not considered terrorist, such as nuclear deterrence, certain police operations, and mass rapes etc. The terror-based definition is therefore too broad.

The definitions of terrorism should be consistent because of the criminal law's moral or normative rather than instrumental function. If definitions of terrorism are drafted inconsistently, they may continue to undermine the moral force of the post-9/11 global legal response. The Secretary-General's High-Level Panel clearly made this point in 2004 when it presented its final report entitled "*A More Secure World: Our Shared Responsibility*."[198] The High-Level Panel expressed concern that the United Nations had failed to achieve the same consistency in state responses to terrorism and non-state conflict as it had with inter-state conflict and the use of military force. It recognised that this lack of consistency not only undermined the practical effectiveness of the international community's strategies to reduce terrorist activity, but also undermined the normative force of its moral stance against the underlying wrongfulness of terrorism: "The United Nations must achieve the same degree of normative strength concerning non-State use of force as it has concerning State use of force. Lack of agreement on a clear and well-known definition undermines the normative and moral stance against terrorism and has stained the United Nations image."[199]

Two years later, the United Nations reiterated its desire for consistent state responses to the international terrorist threat in its 2006 Global Counter-Terrorism Strategy.[200] That document called for 'a strategy to promote comprehensive, co-ordinated and consistent responses, at the national, regional and international levels.'[201] As the

High-Level Panel makes clear, such co-ordination and consistency is not necessary only for the international community to maintain an effective practical campaign against terrorist activity. It is also necessary for the international community to maintain a coherent moral campaign against the underlying wrongfulness of terrorism. The moral coherence of the global response to terrorism is compromised by the laws of some states and not others describing particular conduct as terrorism. This causes confusion and moral uncertainty about the kinds of conduct that amount to terrorism. It undermines the criminal law's ability to denounce or condemn terrorism as morally unacceptable conduct on both a domestic and global level. Different states have different needs, capabilities, and political, legal and ideological contexts. What may work to combat terrorism in one jurisdiction may simply not work in another.[203] At the very least, however, definitions of terrorism should be drafted consistently in jurisdictions with similar legal and parliamentary traditions in order to encourage effective interstate co-operation and to buttress the moral force of the post-9/11 legal response.

References

1. UN Doc. A/8969, Williamson, M. (2009). *Terrorism, War and International Law* (p. 54). England: Ashgate Publishing Limited.
2. *Ibid.*
3. Amnesty International. (2005), (AI Index: MDE 14/009/ 2005). *Iraq in Cold Blood: Abuses by Armed Groups*, Retrieved 2011, October 01 from http://www.amnesty.org/en/library/asset/MDE14/009/2005/en/399c82bd-d4f4-11dd-8a23-d58a49c0d652/mde140092005en.pdf.
4. Second Administrative Reforms Commission, Government of India. (June 2008). *Combating Terrorism: Protecting by Righteousness*, (Eighth Report, Chapter 4). p. 47. Retrieved 2011, October 02 from http://arc.gov.in/8threport/ARC_8thReport_Ch4.pdf.
5. *Ibid.*
6. Pal P. (2006). The New Face of Terrorism in a Globalised Context. In M. Bhattacharya, S. Ghosh, and R. Bhattacharya (Eds.), *Essays on International Terrorism*, (p. 132). Kolkata: Sarat Book Distributors.
7. Zlataric B. (1975). History of International Terrorism and its Legal Control. In M.C. Bassiouni (Ed), *International Terrorism and Political Crimes,* (pp. 474, 478-482). Springfield, Illinois: Charles C Thomas Publisher Ltd.
8. Williamson, M. (2009). *Terrorism, War and International law* (p. 49). England: Ashgate Publishing Limited.
9. Zlataric B. (1975). History of International Terrorism and its Legal Control. In M.C. Bassiouni (Ed), *International Terrorism and Political Crimes,* (pp. 474, 478-482). Springfield, Illinois: Charles C Thomas Publisher Ltd.
10. *Ibid.*
11. *Ibid.*, pp. 481- 482.
12. Walters, F. (1969). *A History of the League of Nations* (p. 599). London: Oxford University Press.
13. *Ibid.*, p. 602.

14. *Ibid*, pp. 244-255.
15. *Ibid.*, p. 604.
16. *Ibid.*, pp. 246, 600.
17. Saul, B. (March 2006). The Legal response of the League of Nations to Terrorism, *Journal of International Criminal Justice*, 4(1), Oxford Journals, Oxford University Press, pp. 78, 81.
18. Nawaz M.K. and Singh G. (1977). Legal Control of International Terrorism. *Indian Journal of International Law. 17*, New Delhi, p. 66 at 67.
19. Article 1.1.
20. Article 2.
21. Schmid, Alex P., & Jongman, Albert J. (1988). Political Terrorism: A New Guide to Actors, Authors, Concepts, Data Bases, Theories and Literature (p. 28). New Brunswick (USA) and London (UK): Transaction Publishers.
22. Alexander, Y. (1976). *International Terrorism: National, Regional and Global Perspectives*. (p. xiv). New York: Praeger Publisher.
23. Hoffman, B. (2006). *Inside Terrorism*. (p. 43). New York: Columbia University Press.
24. Higgins, R. (1997). The General International Law of Terrorism. In Rosalyn Higgins, and M. Flory (Eds.), *Terrorism and International Law*, (p. 28). London: Sweet and Maxwell.
25. Higgins, R. (1997). The General International Law of Terrorism. In Rosalyn Higgins, and M. Flory (Eds.), *Terrorism and International Law* (p. 28). London: Sweet and Maxwell.
26. Richardson L. (2006). *What Terrorist Want: Understanding the Enemy, Granting the Threat*. (p. 19). New York: Random House.
27. Schmid, Alex P. (2004). Terrorism: The Definitional Problem, *Case Western Reserve Journal of International Law, 36(2) and (3)*, Cleveland, p. 408.
28. Terrorism. (2014). In *Encyclopædia Britannica*. Retrieved from http://www.britannica.com/EBchecked/topic/588371/terrorism.

29. Garner, B. A. (2008). *Black's Law Dictionary.* 8th Ed. p. 1512.

30. Garner, B. A. (2008). *Black's Law Dictionary.* 8th Ed. p. 1512.

31. *Chambers 21st Century Dictionary.* (2000). New Delhi: Allied Publishers Limited. p. 458.

32. Oxford Advanced Learner's Dictionary. (2002). New Delhi: Oxford University Press, 6th Ed. p. 1342.

33. Part 1, Section 1. Retrieved October 3, 2011 from http://www.soca.gov.uk/about-soca/library/doc_download/178-terrorism-act-2000-tact.pdf.

34. Retrieved October 3, 2011 from http://www.legislation.gov.uk/ukpga/2006/11/pdfs/ukpga_20060011_en.pdf.

35. Section 83.01, Criminal Code, Canada, R.S.C., 1985, c. C-46, Retrieved October 4, 2011 from http://laws-lois.justice.gc.ca/PDF/C-46.pdf.

36. Criminal Code Amendment (Terrorism) Act 2003, No. 40, 2003, Part 5.3, Division 100.1, Retrieved October 5, 2011 from http://www.comlaw.gov.au/Details/C2004A01125.

37. Section 5(1)(b) of the New Zealand Terrorism Suppression Act, 2002, Retrieved October 6, 2011 from http://www.legislation.govt.nz/act/public/2002/0034/latest/DLM151491.html.

38. French Penal Code, Title II – OF Terrorism, Chapter I – of acts of Terrorism, Article 421-1. Retrieved October 4, 2011 from http://www.legifrance.gouv.fr/content/download/1957/13715/version/4/file/Code_33.pdf.

39. Department of Army and Department of Navy, United States of America (As amended through 15th August, 2012). Department of Defence Dictionary of Military and Associated Terms, p. 313. Retrieved August 17, 2012 from http://www.dtic.mil/doctrine/new_pubs/jp1_02.pdf.

40. U.S Code, title 22, chapter 38, para. 2656f(d). Retrieved October 6th, 2011 from http://www.uscode.house.gov/download/pls/22C38.txt.

41. Part – I, Section 2331, Retrieved October 4, 2011 from http://uscode.house.gov/download/pls/18C113B.txt.
42. Title 18 -- Crimes and Criminal Procedure, Part I – Crimes, Chapter 113B – Terrorism, Section 2331 of US Code. Pub. L. 102-572, title X, Section 1003 (a) (3), Oct. 29, 1992, 106 Stat. 4521; amended Pub. L. 107-56, title VIII, Section 802 (a), Oct. 26, 2001, 115 Stat. 376.). Retrieved October 7, 2011 from http://uscode.house.gov/uscodecgi/fast web.exe ?getdoc +uscview+t 17t20+1097+0+ +% 28terrorism% 29%20%20AND%20% 28USC%20w%2 F10%20% 282331% 29%29%3ACITE.
43. Title 18 – *Crimes and Criminal Procedure*, Part II – Criminal Procedure, Chapter 204 – Rewards for Information Concerning Terrorist Acts and Espionage, Section 3077 of US Code. Retrieved October 8, 2011 from http://www.law.cornell.edu/uscode/text/18/3077.
44. G.A. Res. 49/60, U.N. GAOR, 49th Sess., 84th mtg., Supp. No. 49, U.N. Doc. A/49/60, (1994); *Declaration on Measures to Eliminate International Terrorism*, adopted on 9th December, 1994. Retrieved October 9, 2011 from http://www.un.org/documents/ga/res/49/a49r060.htm.
45. *UN G.A. Resolution 50/53 of 1995*, U.N. Doc. A/RES/50/53, adopted on 29th January, 1996. Retrieved October 9, 2011 from http://www.un.org/en/ga/search/view_doc.asp? symbol =A/RES/50/53&Lang=E.
46. *UN G.A. Resolution 51/210 of 1996,* U.N. Doc. A/RES/51/210, adopted on 16th January, 1997. Retrieved October 10, 2011 from http://www.un.org/en/ga/search/view_doc.asp?symbol=A/RES/51/210&Lang=E.
47. UN G.A. Resolution 52/165 of 1997, U.N. Doc. A/RES/52/165, adopted on 19th January, 1998. Retrieved October 10, 2011 from http://www.un.org/en/ga/search/view_doc.asp?symbol=A/RES/52/165&Lang=E.
48. UN G.A. Resolution 53/108 of 1998, U.N. Doc. A/RES/53/108, adopted on 26th January, 1999. Retrieved October 10, 2011 from http://www.un.org/en/ga/search/view_doc.asp?symbol=A/RES/53/108&Lang=E.

49. UN G.A. Resolution 54/110 of 1999, U.N. Doc. A/RES/54/110, adopted on 2nd February, 2000. Retrieved October 11, 2011 from http://www.un.org/en/ga/search/view_doc.asp?symbol=A/RES/54/110&Lang=E.

50. UN G.A. Resolution 55/158 of 2000, U.N. Doc. A/RES/55/158, adopted on 30th January, 2001. Retrieved October 11, 2011 from http://www.un.org/en/ga/search/view_doc.asp?symbol=A/RES/55/158&Lang=E.

51. UN G.A. Resolution 56/88 of 2001, U.N. Doc. A/RES/56/88, adopted on 24th January, 2002. Retrieved October 11, 2011 from http://www.un.org/en/ga/search/view_doc. asp?symbol =A/RES/56/88&Lang=E.

52. UN G.A. Resolution 57/27 of 2002, U.N. Doc. A/RES/57/27, adopted on 15th January, 2003. Retrieved October 12, 2011 from http://www.un.org/en/ga/search/view_doc.asp?symbol=A/RES/57/27&Lang=E.

53. UN G.A. Resolution 58/81 of 2003, U.N. Doc. A/RES/58/81, adopted on 8th January, 2004. Retrieved October 12, 2011 from http://www.un.org/en/ga/search/view_doc.asp?symbol=A/RES/58/81&Lang=E.

54. UN G.A. Resolution 59/46 of 2004, U.N. Doc. A/RES/59/46, adopted on 16th December, 2004. Retrieved October 13, 2011 from http://www.un.org/en/ga/search/view_doc.asp? symbol =A/RES/59/46&Lang=E.

55. UN G.A. Resolution 60/43 of 2005, U.N. Doc. A/RES/60/43, adopted on 6th January, 2006. Retrieved October 13, 2011 from http://www.un.org/en/ga/search/view_doc.asp? symbol =A/RES/59/46&Lang=E.

56. UN G.A. Resolution 61/40 of 2006, U.N. Doc. A/RES/61/40, adopted on 18th December, 2006. Retrieved October 14, 2011 from http://www.un.org/en/ga/search/view_doc.asp? symbol =A/RES/61/40&Lang=E.

57. UN G.A. Resolution 62/71 of 2007, U.N. Doc. A/RES/62/71, adopted on 8th January, 2008. Retrieved October 14, 2011 from http://www.un.org/en/ga/search/view_doc.asp? symbol =A/RES/62/71&Lang=E.

58. UN G.A. Resolution 63/129 of 2008, U.N. Doc. A/RES/63/129, adopted on 15th January, 2009. Retrieved October 15, 2011 from http://www.un.org/en/ga/search/view_doc.asp?symbol=A/RES/63/129&Lang=E.
59. UN G.A. Resolution 64/118 of 2009, U.N. Doc. A/RES/64/118, adopted on 15th January, 2010. Retrieved October 15, 2011 from http://www.un.org/en/ga/search/view_doc.asp?symbol=A/RES/64/118.
60. UN G.A. Resolution 65/34 of 2010, U.N. Doc. A/RES/65/34, adopted on 10th January, 2011. Retrieved October 16, 2011 from http://www.un.org/en/ga/search/view_doc.asp?symbol=A/RES/65/34.
61. UN G.A. Resolution 66/105 of 2011, U.N. Doc. A/RES/66/105, adopted on 13th January, 2012. Retrieved October 16, 2011 from http://www.un.org/en/ga/search/view_doc.asp?symbol=%20A/RES/66/105.
62. UN G.A. Resolution 67/99 of 2012, U.N. Doc. A/RES/67/99, adopted on 14th January, 2013. Retrieved October 16, 2011 from http://www.un.org/en/ga/search/view_doc.asp?symbol=A/RES/67/99.
63. Report of The Secretary-General of the United Nations for decision by Heads of State and Government in September 2005, *In larger freedom: towards development, security and human rights for all*, Fifty-ninth session, A/59/2005, p. 26. Retrieved October 17, 2011 from http://daccess-dds-ny.un.org/doc/UNDOC/GEN/N05/270/78/PDF/N0527078.pdf?OpenElement
64. Annex II to Measures to eliminate international terrorism, Report of the Working Group. U.N. Doc A/C.6/55/L2. Adopted on 19th October, 2000, Retrieved October 17, 2011 from http://daccess-dds-ny.un.org/doc/UNDOC/LTD/N00/697/77/PDF/N0069777.pdf?OpenElement.
65. U.N. Economic and Social. Council, Commission on Human Rights, Report of the Special Rapporteur on the Promotion and Protection of Human Rights and Fundamental Freedoms While Countering Terrorism. U.N. Doc. E/CN.4/2006/98, 28th September, 2005, p 9, para 28. Retrieved October 17,

2011 from http://daccess-dds-ny.un.org/doc/UNDOC/GEN/G05/168/84/PDF/G0516884.pdf?OpenElement.

66. U.N. Security Council Resolution 1373 of 2001, S/RES/1373/2001, adopted by Security Council on 28th September, 2001, Retrieved October 18, 2011 from http://www.un.org/ga/search/view_doc.asp?symbol=S/RES/1373(2001).

67. U.N. Security Council Resolution 1566 of 2004, S/RES/1566/2004, adopted by Security Council on 8th October, 2004, Retrieved October 17, 2011 from http://www.un.org/ga/search/view_doc.asp?symbol=S/RES/1566(2004).

68. United Nations General Assembly Resolution A/RES/52/164, adopted on 9th January, 1998. Retrieved October 18, 2011 from http://treaties.un.org/doc/db/Terrorism/english-18-9.pdf.

69. Adopted by the General Assembly of the United Nations in resolution 54/109 on 9th December 1999. Retrieved October 17, 2011 from http://www.un.org/law/cod/finterr.htm.

70. Adopted on 14th September, 2005. Retrieved October 18, 2011 from http://treaties.un.org/doc/db/Terrorism/english-18-15.pdf.

71. Signed at Kathmandu on 4th November, 1987. Retrieved October 18, 2011 from http://www.unhcr.org/refworld/pdfid/3dd8ab3a4.pdf.

72. Signed at Cairo, Egypt on 22nd April, 1998. Retrieved October 19, 2011 from https://www.unodc.org/tldb/pdf/conv_arab_terrorism.en.pdf.

73. *Ibid.*

74. Signed at Minsk on 4th June, 1999. Retrieved October 19, 2011 from http://treaties.un.org/doc/db/Terrorism/csi-english.pdf.

75. Adopted at Ouagadougou on 1st July, 1999. Retrieved October 20, 2011 from http://www.oicun.org/7/38/

76. *Ibid.*

77. Adopted at Algiers on 14th July, 1999. Retrieved October 20, 2011 from http://treaties.un.org/doc/db/Terrorism/OAU-english.pdf.

78. Council Framework Decision on combating terrorism, adopted on 13th June 2002. (2002/475/JHA). Retrieved October 20, 2011 fromhttp://eur-lex.europa.eu/LexUriServ/LexUri Serv.do?uri=OJ:L:2002: 164:0003:0003: EN:PDF
79. Draft Model Legislation on Measures to Combat Terrorism. Criminal Law Section, Legal and Constitutional Affairs Division, Commonwealth Secretariat, September 2002, Part I. Retrieved October 21, 2011 from http://www. the common wealth.org/shared_asp_files/uploadedfiles/%7B32AF830D-F83A-4432-8051-750C789531A5%7D_ final_ terrorism_ law.pdf
80. *Ibid.*
81. Draft comprehensive convention on international terrorism (CCIT) presented by India in the year 1996 to the United Nations. Retrieved October 21, 2011 from http://www.satp.org/satporgtp/countries/india/document/papers/India_IntConv.htm
82. Section 2(h) of Terrorist Affected Areas (Special Courts) Act, 1984.
83. Section 3(1) of Terrorist and Disruptive Activities (Prevention) Act, 1985.
84. Section 2(1)(y) of Indian National Security Guard Act, 1986.
85. Section 3(1) of Prevention of Terrorism Act, 2002.
86. Section 15 of Unlawful Activities (Prevention) Amendment Act, 2004.
87. Section 15 of Unlawful Activities (Prevention) Amendment Act, 2008.
88. Published in the Gazette of India, Extra. Part II, Section 1, dated January 4, 2013.
89. Section 15 of Unlawful Activities (Prevention) Amendment Act, 2008.
90. (1994) 3 SCC 569.
91. *State v. Nalini and Others s*, (1999)5 SCC 253.
92. AIR 1994 SC 2623: 1994(4) SCC 602.

93. 1998(4) SCC 494.
94. Retrieved October 30, 2011 from http://www.legislation.gov.uk/ukpga/2008/28/pdfs/ukpga_20080028_en.pdf.
95. Schmid, Alex P., & Jongman, Albert J. (1988). Political Terrorism: A New Guide to Actors, Authors, Concepts, Data Bases, Theories and Literature (p. 28). New Brunswick (USA) & London (UK): Transaction Publishers.
96. Bassiouni, M. Cherif. (2001). *International Terrorism; Multilateral Conventions (1937–2001).* (pp. 16-17). Ardsley, New York: Transnational Publishers.
97. Bassiouni, M.C. (1988). *A Policy-oriented Inquiry of 'International Terrorism.* In M. Cherif Bassiouni (Ed.), Legal Responses to International Terrorism: U.S. Procedural Aspects, (pp. xv-xvi). Dordrecht, Boston and London: Martinus Nijhoff Publishers, 1988.
98. *1954 ILC Draft Code of Offences against the Peace and Security of Mankind* (Part I), in ILC 6th Session Report (3 June–28 Jul 1954), UN Doc A/2693. Retrieved November 01, 2011 from http://untreaty.un.org/ilc/texts/instruments/english/draft%20articles/7_3_1954.pdf.
99. UN G.A. Resolution 36/106, U.N. Doc. A/RES/36/106, adopted on 10th December, 1981. Retrieved November 01, 2011 from http://daccess-dds-ny.un.org/doc/RESOLUTION/GEN/NR0/407/32/IMG/NR040732.pdf?OpenElement
100. Year Book of the International Law Commission, 1991, Volume 1, Summary records of the meetings of the forty-third session, 29th April–19th July, 1991. Retrieved November 01, 2011 from http://untreaty.un.org/ilc/publications/yearbooks/Ybkvolumes%28e%29/ILC_1991_v1_e.pdf.
101. Report of the International Law Commission on the work of its forty-seventh session, 2nd May–21st July 1995, Official Records of the General Assembly, Fiftieth session, UNGAOR Supp 10, UN Doc A/50/10, p. 28, para 105-111. Retrieved November 02, 2011 from http://untreaty.un.org/ilc//documentation/english/A_50_10.pdf.
102. Report of the International Law Commission on the work of its forty-eighth session, 6th May–26th July 1996, Official

Records of the General Assembly, Fiftieth-first session, UNGAOR Supp 10, UN Doc A/51/10. page 17, para 47-48. Retrieved November 02, 2011 from http://untreaty.un.org/ilc/documentation/english/A_51_10.pdf.

103. Report of the International Law Commission on the work of its forty-seventh session, 2nd May – 21st July 1995, Official Records of the General Assembly, Fiftieth session, UNGAOR Supp 10, UN Doc A/50/10, chapter II(2), para 27-143. Retrieved November 02, 2011 from http://untreaty.un.org/ilc//documentation/english/A_50_10.pdf.

104. Press Release, Security Council, Security Council Acts Unanimously to Adopt Resolution Strongly Condemning Terrorism as One of Most Serious Threats to Peace, U.N. Doc. SC/8214 (Oct. 8th, 2004), Retrieved November 03, 2011 from http://www.un.org/News/Press/docs/2004/sc8214.doc.htm.

105. Security Council Press Release, 4413rd Meeting (AM), Press Release SC/7207, 12th November 2001. Retrieved November 03, 2011 from http://www.un.org/News/Press/docs/2001/sc7207.doc.htm.

106. Security Council Press Release, 4453rd Meeting (AM and PM), Press Release SC/7276, 18th January 2002. Retrieved November 04, 2011 from http://www.un.org/News/Press/docs/2002/SC7276.doc.htm.

107. Security Council Press Release, 4512th and 4513th Meetings (AM & PM), Press Release SC/7361, 15th April 2002. Retrieved November 04, 2011 from http://www.un.org/News/Press/docs/2002/SC7361.doc.htm.

108. Para 9 of U.N. Security Council Resolution 1566 of 2004, S/RES/1566/2004, adopted by Security Council on 8th October, 2004, Retrieved November 05, 2011 from http://www.un.org/ga/search/view_doc.asp?symbol=S/RES/1566(2004).

109. G.A. Res. 49/60, U.N. GAOR, 49th Session., 84th mtg., Supp. No. 49, U.N. Doc. A/49/60, (1994); *Declaration on Measures to Eliminate International Terrorism*, adopted on 9th December, 1994. Annexed Declaration, para. 3 Retrieved November 06, 2011 from http://www.un.org/documents/ga/res/49/a49r060.htm.

110. Special Rapporteur on the Protection and Promotion of Human Rights While Countering Terrorism, *Report of the Special Rapporteur on the Protection and Promotion of Human Rights While Countering Terrorism*, Economic and Social Council, Commission on Human Rights, UN Doc. E/CN.4/2006/98, para 50, adopted on 28th December, 2005, Retrieved November 08, 2011 from http://daccess-dds-ny.un.org/doc/UNDOC/GEN/G05/168/84/PDF/G0516884.pdf?OpenElement.

111. U.N. Security Council Resolution 1566 of 2004, S/RES/1566/2004, adopted by Security Council on 8th October, 2004, para 4-6. Retrieved November 10, 2011 from http://www.un.org/ga/search/view_doc.asp?symbol=S/RES/1566(2004).

112. *Ibid.*

113. International Convention for the Suppression of the Financing of Terrorism, 1999. Adopted by the General Assembly of the United Nations in resolution 54/109 on 9th December 1999, Article 2(1), 4. Retrieved November 11, 2011 from http://www.un.org/law/cod/finterr.htm.

114. *Ibid.*

115. *Report of the Ad Hoc Committee established by General Assembly Resolution 51/210 of 17th December,* 1996, Fifth Session (12 – 23 February 2001), U.N. GAOR, 56th Sess., Supp. No. 37, U.N. Doc. A/56/37 (2001). Retrieved November 14, 2011.

116. Adopted by the General Assembly of the United Nations in resolution 54/109 on 9th December 1999. Retrieved November 15, 2011 from http://www.un.org/law/cod/finterr.htm.

117. *Report of the Ad Hoc Committee established by General Assembly Resolution 51/210 of 17th December 1996, Sixth Session (28 January–1 February 2002), U.N. GAOR, 57th Sess., Supp. No. 37, U.N. Doc. A/57/37 (2002). Retrieved November 15, 2011 from http://daccess-dds-ny.un.org/doc/UNDOC/GEN/N02/248/17/PDF/N0224817.pdf? OpenElement.*

118. *Ibid.*

119. Goswami, A. (2002). *Combating Terrorism: The Legal Challenge*

(p. 25). New Delhi: Har Anand Publication.

120. *State v. Nalini and others* , (1999) 5 SCC 253.

121. Second Administrative Reforms Commission, Government of India. (June 2008). *Combating Terrorism: Protecting by Righteousness*, (Eighth Report, Chapter 4). p.47. Retrieved November 18, 2011 from http://arc.gov.in/8threport/ARC_8th Report_Ch4.pdf.

122. Law Commission of India, One seventy third report on *Prevention of Terrorism Bill, 2000,* April, 2000. Retrieved November 17, 2011.

123. AIR 2004 SC 456.

124. *Ibid.*

125. Second Administrative Reforms Commission, Government of India. (June 2008). *Combating Terrorism: Protecting by Righteousness*, (Eighth Report, Chapter 4). p. 51. Retrieved November 20, 2011.

126. *Ibid.*

127. Reuven Y. (2006). Defining Terrorism: The Evolution of Terrorism as a Legal Concept in International Law and its Influence on Definitions in Domestic Legislation, *Boston College International and Comparative Law Review*, *29*(1) p. 23. Retrieved November 25, 2011.

128. Tiefenbrun, S. (2003). A Semiotic Approach to a Legal Definition of Terrorism. *International Law Students Association Journal of International and Comparative Law*, *9*, p. 357, at 365. Retrieved November 30, 2011 from http:/ /www.pegc.us/archive/Journals/tiefenbrun_terroism_def.pdf.

129. *Ibid.*

130. UN High-Level Panel on Threats, Challenges and Change, *A More Secure World: Our Shared Responsibility* (UN, December 2004), p.l 52. Retrieved November 30, 2011 from https:// www.un.org/secureworld/report2.pdf.

131. *Ibid.*

132. Wilkins, Burleigh T (1992). *Terrorism and Collective Responsibility* (p. 2). London : Routledge.

133. Committee on Reforms of Criminal Justice System, Government of India, Ministry of Home Affairs. (March 2003). Report, at 213. Retrieved December 02, 2011.

134. *Ibid.*, at 214.

135. *Ibid*, at 214.

136. *Ibid.*, at 294.

137. Hoffman, Bruce (2006). *Inside Terrorism* (2nd ed.). New York: Columbia University Press, p. 31.

138. Tiefenbrun, S. (2003). A Semiotic Approach to a Legal Definition of Terrorism. *International Law Students Association Journal of International and Comparative Law*, *9*, p. 357, at 362. Retrieved December 03, 2011.

139. Bassiouni, M. Cherif. (2001). *International Terrorism; Multilateral Conventions (1937 – 2001).* (p. 29). Ardsley, New York: Transnational Publishers.

140. Bhattacharya, S. (2007). *Terrorism and Moral Questions* (pp. 17-18). Kolkata: Sarat Book Distributors.

141. Tiefenbrun, S. (2003). A Semiotic Approach to a Legal Definition of Terrorism. *International Law Students Association Journal of International and Comparative Law*, *9*, p. 357, at 364. Retrieved December 06, 2011 from http://www.pegc.us/archive/Journals/tiefenbrun_terroism_def.pdf.

142. Brian. J.(1975). International Terrorism: A New Mode of Conflict. In David Carlton, and Carlo Schaerf (Eds.), *International Terrorism and World Security*, (p. 16). London: Croom Helm.

143. Tiefenbrun, S. (2003). A Semiotic Approach to a Legal Definition of Terrorism. *International Law Students Association Journal of International and Comparative Law*, *9*, p. 357, at 364. Retrieved December 06, 2011.

144. Primoratz, I. (2004). What is Terrorism? In Igor Primoratz (Ed.), *Terrorism: The Philosophical Issues*, (pp. 15-27). New York: Palgrave Macmillan.

145. Tiefenbrun, S. (2003). A Semiotic Approach to a Legal Definition of Terrorism. *International Law Students*

Association Journal of International and Comparative Law, 9, p. 357, at 364. Retrieved December 06, 2011.

146. Goswami, A. (2002). *Combating Terrorism, the Legal Challenge.* (pp. 34-35). New Delhi: Har Anand Publications.

147. *Nazir Khan and Others.* v. *State of Delhi,* AIR 2003 SC 4427.

148. The Definition of Terrorism, A Report by Lord Carlile of Berriew Q.C.; Independent Reviewer of Terrorism Legislation, Presented to Parliament by the Secretary of State for the Home Department, By Command of Her Majesty, United Kingdom, March 2007. Retrieved December 20, 2011 from http://www.official-documents.gov.uk/document/cm70/7052/7052.pdf.

149. *Report of the UN Policy Working Group on the UN and Terrorism, 2002. A/57/273-S/2002/875, Retrieved December 22, 2011.*

150. *Secretary-General's High-Level Panel on Threats, Challenges and Change,* More Secure World: Our Shared Responsibility, Report of the Secretary-General's High-Level Panel on Threats, Challenges and Change, U.N. Doc. A/59/565 (December 2, 2004). Retrieved December 22, 2011.

151. *Ibid.* p., Para 157.

152. Secretary-General's *High-Level Panel on Threats, Challenges and Change, More Secure World: Our Shared Responsibility,* Report of the Secretary-General's High-Level Panel on Threats, Challenges and Change, Page 49, Para 164, U.N. Doc. A/59/565 (December 2, 2004). Retrieved December 23, 2011 from http://www.un.org/secureworld/report.pdf.

153. *G.A. Res. 60/1, Resolution* adopted by the General Assembly, pp. 81-91, Page 22, U.N. Doc A/RES/60/1 (October 24, 2005). Retrieved December 24, 2011 from http://unpan1.un.org/intradoc/groups/public/documents/un/unpan021752.pdf.

154. *Euro-Mediterranean Code of Conduct on Countering Terrorism (2005),* Retrieved December 27, 2011 from http://www.eeas.europa.eu/euromed/summit1105/index_en.htm.

155. UN Commission on Human Rights, "*Report of the Special Rapporteur on the promotion and protection of human rights*

and fundamental freedoms while countering terrorism, Martin Scheinin," E/CN.4/2006/98, December 28, 2005, Retrieved December 28, 2011 from http://www.coe.int/t/e/legal_affairs/legal_cooperation/fight_against_terrorism/3_CODEXTER/Working_Documents/2006/Sheinin%20E-CN.4-2006-98.pdf.

156. *Ibid.*
157. Wolman, Benjamin B. (1989). *Dictionary of Behavioural Science* (2nd Ed.). New York: Academic Press, p. 79.
158. Garner, B. A. (2008). *Black's Law Dictionary.* 8th Ed. p. 399.
159. Crime. (2011). In *Encyclopædia Britannica.* Retrieved December 28, 2011.
160. Schmid, Alex P. (2004). *Frame works for conceptualising terrorism*', *Terrorism and political violence. 16(2).* UK: Routledge. pp. 197-221.
161. Garner, B.A. (2008). *Black's Law Dictionary.* 8th Ed. p. 1614.
162. *Chambers 21st Century Dictionary*. (2000). New Delhi: Allied Publishers Limited. p. 1597.
163. Garner, B. A. (2008). *Black's Law Dictionary.* 8th Ed. p. 1615.
164. *Chambers 21st Century Dictionary*. (2000). New Delhi: Allied Publishers Limited. p. 595.
165. Magill, Frank N. (1996). Insurgency. In *International Encyclopaedia of Government and Politics* (Vol. 1, p. 642), Chicago: Fitzroy Dearborn Publishers.
166. Garner, B. A. (2008). *Black's Law Dictionary.* 8th Ed. p. 823.
167. Chambers 21st Century Dictionary. (2000). New Delhi: Allied Publishers Limited. p. 706.
168. Arnold, T. E. (1988). *The violence formula: why people lend sympathy and support to terrorism.* (p. 193). Lexington, Massachusetts: Lexington Books.
169. *Ibid.*, p. 111.

170. *UN G.A. Resolution 34/145*, U.N. Doc. A/RES/34/145, adopted on 17th December, 1979. Para 11. Retrieved January 05, 2012 from http://www.un.org/documents/ga/res/34/a34res145.pdf.

171. *UN G.A. Resolution 38/130*, U.N. Doc. A/RES/38/130, adopted on 19th December, 1983. Para 6. Retrieved January 05, 2012 from http://www.un.org/documents/ga/res/38/a38r130.htm.

172. *UN G.A. Resolution 40/61*, U.N. Doc. A/RES/40/61, adopted on 9th December, 1985. Para 8. Retrieved January 05, 2012 from http://www.un.org/documents/ga/res/40/a40r061.htm.

173. *UN G.A. Resolution 42/159*, U.N. Doc. A/RES/42/159, adopted on 7th December, 1987. Para5. Retrieved January 05, 2012 from http://www.un.org/documents/ga/res/42/a42r159.htm.

174. *UN G.A. Resolution 44/29*, U.N. Doc. A/RES/44/29, adopted on 4th December, 1989. Para4. Retrieved January 05, 2012 from http://www.un.org/documents/ga/res/44/a44r029.htm.

175. *UN G.A. Resolution 46/51*, U.N. Doc. A/RES/46/51, adopted on 9th December, 1991. Para16. Retrieved January 05, 2012 from http://www.un.org/documents/ga/res/46/a46r051.htm.

176. *UN G.A. Resolution 49/60*, U.N. Doc. A/RES/49/60, adopted on 9th December, 1994. Retrieved January 05, 2012 from http://www.un.org/documents/ga/res/49/a49r060.htm.

177. *Ibid.*

178. *UN G.A. Resolution 55/158,* U.N. Doc. A/RES/55/158, adopted on 30th January, 2001. Para 2. Retrieved January 05, 2012 from http://daccess-dds-ny.un.org/doc/UNDOC/GEN/N00/568/87/PDF/N0056887.pdf?OpenElement.

179. *UN G.A. Resolution 54/110,* U.N. Doc. A/RES/54/110, adopted on 2nd February, 2000. Para 2. Retrieved January 06, 2012 from http://daccess-dds-ny.un.org/doc/UNDOC/GEN/N00/251/34/PDF/N0025134.pdf?OpenElement.

180. *UN G.A. Resolution 53/108*, U.N. Doc. A/RES/53/108, adopted on 2nd February, 2000. Para2. Retrieved January 06, 2012 from http://daccess-dds-ny.un.org/doc/UNDOC/

GEN/N99/762/67/PDF/N9976267.pdf?OpenElement.

181. *UN G.A. Resolution 52/165,* U.N. Doc. A/RES/52/165, adopted on 19th January, 1998. Para 2. Retrieved January 06, 2012 from http://daccess-dds-ny.un.org/doc/UNDOC/GEN/N98/761/59/PDF/N9876159.pdf?OpenElement.

182. *UN G.A. Resolution 51/210*, U.N. Doc. A/RES/51/210, adopted on 17th December, 1996. Para 2. Retrieved January 06, 2012 from http://www.un.org/documents/ga/res/51/a51r210.htm.

183. *UN G.A. Resolution 50/53*, U.N. Doc. A/RES/50/53, adopted on 11th December, 1995. Para 2. http://www.un.org/documents/ga/res/50/a50r053.htm.

184. *UN G.A. Resolution 56/1,* U.N. Doc. A/RES/56/1, adopted on 12th September, 2001. Retrieved January 06, 2012 from http://www.un.org/documents/ga/docs/56/agresolution.htm.

185. *UN G.A. Resolution 46/51*, U.N. Doc. A/RES/46/51, adopted on 9th December, 1991. Retrieved January 07, 2012 from http://www.un.org/documents/ga/res/46/a46r051.htm.

186. *UN G.A. Resolution 49/60*, U.N. Doc. A/RES/49/60, adopted on 9th December, 1994. Retrieved January 07, 2012 from http://www.un.org/documents/ga/res/49/a49r060.htm.

187. *UN G.A. Resolution 56/88*, U.N. Doc. A/RES/56/88, adopted on 24th January, 2002. Retrieved January 08, 2012 from http://www.treasury.gov/resource-center/sanctions/Terrorism-Proliferation-Narcotics/Documents/A-RES-56-88.pdf.

188. *Ibid*, para 7.

189. *UN G.A. Resolution 57/27*, U.N. Doc. A/RES/57/27, adopted on 15th January, 2003. Retrieved January 08, 2012 from http://www.treasury.gov/resource-center/sanctions/Terrorism-Proliferation-Narcotics/Documents/A-RES-57-27.pdf.

190. *UN G.A. Resolution 58/81*, U.N. Doc. A/RES/58/81, adopted on 8th January, 2004. Retrieved January 08, 2012 from http://www.worldlii.org/int/other/UNGARsn/2003/136.pdf.

191. *UN G.A. Resolution 59/46*, U.N. Doc. A/RES/59/46, adopted on 16th December, 2004. Retrieved January 09, 2012 from

http://daccess-dds-ny.un.org/doc/UNDOC/GEN/N04/479/02/PDF/N0447902.pdf? Open Element.

192. *S.C. Resolution 1368,* U.N. Doc. S/RES/1368, Para 3, adopted on 12th September, 2001. Retrieved January 09, 2012 from http://daccess-dds-ny.un.org/doc/UNDOC/GEN/N01/533/82/PDF/N0153382.pdf?OpenElement.

193. *S.C. Resolution 1373*, U.N. Doc. S/RES/1373, adopted on 28th September, 2001. Retrieved January 09, 2012 from http://daccess-dds-ny.un.org/doc/UNDOC/GEN/N01/557/43/PDF/N0155743.pdf?OpenElement.

194. *S.C. Resolution 1377,* U.N. Doc. S/RES/1377, adopted on 12th November, 2001. Retrieved January 09, 2012.

195. *S.C. Resolution 1456*, U.N. Doc. S/RES/1456, adopted on 20th January, 2003. Retrieved January 10, 2012.

196. *S.C. Resolution 1566,* U.N. Doc. S/RES/1566, adopted on 8th October, 2004. Retrieved January 10, 2012.

197. *S.C. Resolution 1636,* U.N. Doc. S/RES/1636, adopted on 31st October, 2005. Retrieved January 10, 2012.

198. *S.C. Resolution 1644,* U.N. Doc. S/RES/1644, adopted on 15th December, 2005. Retrieved January 11, 2012 from http:/www.un.org/ga/search/view_doc.asp?symbol=S/RES/1644%282005%29.

199. *S.C. Resolution 1664,* U.N. Doc. S/RES/1664, adopted on 29th March, 2006. Retrieved January 11, 2012 from http://www.un.org/ga/search/view_doc.asp?symbol=S/RES/1664%282006%29.

200. *S.C. Resolution 1735,* U.N. Doc. S/RES/1735, adopted on 22nd December, 2006. Retrieved January 11, 2012 from http://www.un.org/ga/search/view_doc.asp?symbol=S/RES/1735%282006%29.

201. *S.C. Resolution 1757*, U.N. Doc. S/RES/1757, adopted on 30th May, 2007. Retrieved January 12, 2012 from http://www.un.org/ga/search/view_doc.asp?symbol=S/RES/1757%282007%29.

202. *S.C. Resolution 1822,* U.N. Doc. S/RES/1822, adopted on

30th June, 2008. Retrieved January 12, 2012 from http://www.un.org/ga/search/view_doc.asp?symbol=S/RES/1822%282008%29.

203. *S.C. Resolution 1852*, U.N. Doc. S/RES/1852, adopted on 17th December, 2008. Retrieved January 12, 2012 from http://www.un.org/ga/search/view_doc.asp?symbol=S/RES/1852%282008%29.

204. *S.C. Resolution 1904*, U.N. Doc. S/RES/1904, adopted on 17th December, 2009. Retrieved January 12, 2012 from http://www.un.org/ga/search/view_doc.asp?symbol=S/RES/1904%282009%29.

205. *S.C. Resolution 1963,* U.N. Doc. S/RES/1963, adopted on 20th December, 2010. Retrieved January 13, 2012 from http://www.un.org/ga/search/view_doc.asp?symbol=S/RES/1963%282010%29.

206. *S.C. Resolution 1989*, U.N. Doc. S/RES/1989, adopted on 17th June, 2011. Retrieved January 13, 2012 from http://www.un.org/ga/search/view_doc.asp?symbol=S/RES/1989%282011%29.

207. *S.C. Resolution 2083,* U.N. Doc. S/RES/2083, adopted on 17th December, 2012. Retrieved January 13, 2013 from http://www.un.org/ga/search/view_doc.asp?symbol=S/RES/2083%282012%29.

208. *Hitendra Vishnu Thakur* v. *State of Maharashtra* 1994(4) SCC 602.

209. Special Rapporteur on the Protection and Promotion of Human Rights While Countering Terrorism, *Report of the Special Rapporteur on the Protection and Promotion of Human Rights While Countering Terrorism*, UN G.A. Resolution A/RES/64/211, para 27-28, adopted on 3rd August, 2009. last visited on.

210. Oxford Advanced Learner's Dictionary. (2002). New Delhi: Oxford University Press, Indian Edition, 6th Ed. p. 1403.

211. Schmid, Alex P., and Jongman, Albert J. (1988). Political Terrorism: A New Guide to Actors, Authors, Concepts, Data

Bases, Theories and Literature (p. 39). New Brunswick (USA) and London (UK): Transaction Publishers.

212. Laqueur, W. (1999). *The New Terrorism, Fanaticism and the Arms of Mass Destruction* (p. 28). Oxford: Oxford University Press.

213. Schmid, Alex P., and Jongman, Albert J. (1988). Political Terrorism: A New Guide to Actors, Authcrs, Concepts, Data Bases, Theories and Literature (pp. 39-59). New Brunswick (USA) and London (UK): Transaction Publishers.

214. *Hitendra Vishnu Thakur* v. *State of Maharastra*, 1994(4) SCC 602.

215. UN High-Level Panel on Threats, Challenges and Change, *A More Secure World: Our Shared Responsibility* (UN, Dec 2004). Retrieved January 30, 2012.

216. *Ibid.*, p. 51.

217. *UN G.A. Resolution 60/288*, U.N. Doc. A/RES/60/288, adopted on 20th September, 2006. Preamble. Retrieved January 30, 2012.

218. *Ibid.*, Preamble.

219. Ramraj, Victor V. (2012). The Impossibility of Global Anti-Terrorism Law? In Victor V. Ramraj, Michael Hor, Kent Roach, and George Williams (Ed.), *Global Anti-Terrorism Law and Policy,* (p.44). Cambridge: Cambridge University Press.

V
CONCLUSION

It can be concluded by saying that there is a core 'definition of terrorism' at international law that provides guidance to states enacting terrorism legislation, but that to have an effect, states must look to international law and accept its guidance. Although the four domestic definitions are substantively similar to the international definition, all states should treat the international law definitional jurisprudence as setting a minimum level, not a maximum. The international definition of terrorism is destined to develop very slowly, and states need to tailor their legislation to specific national circumstances and respond to threats. The ease with which terrorists can cross borders means states cannot protect themselves simply by enacting and enforcing domestic legislation proscribing terrorism within their borders. Rather, every state must have legislation denying terrorists safe havens and safe places of operation. An established minimum international law definition of terrorism that informs states' domestic criminal law is required to ensure a baseline of consistency and to facilitate international co-operation. The core definition identified in this Article provides that minimum as well as a yardstick against which to measure states' legislation. The existence of a definition of terrorism is important. It shapes states' understanding of the problem, delimits their responses to it, and helps to distinguish lawful from unlawful responses. The perceived absence of an accepted international law definition is said by some largely to explain the inadequacy of international law's ability to combat terrorism. The absence of an internationally accepted definition of terrorism has led to international lawlessness and unilateral vigilantism.

The production of a set of definitions, i.e., of a typology of terrorism instead of a general and monolithic definition, can solve those two problems. It can take up the challenge of relativism by taking into account the diversity of terrorism. Terrorism can be judged in an objective and detailed way precisely because of such a typology. It can reach a wide agreement only if it replaces the impossible quest for a single definition with the search for a precise and detailed set of definitions. Terrorism ought to be strictly defined. It is too central a concept to the moral understanding of our contemporary world to remain obscure. Attempts to avoid its definition in terms of targetting non-combatants are terminologically evasive and unhelpful in understanding the phenomenon, and they quickly lose touch with common usage and intuitions.

It is, therefore, perhaps time to abandon the quest for a universal definition of terrorism and consider whether this time would be better spent creating a series of definitions reflecting the differing motivations of terrorist groups. This would certainly supply leaders in counter-terrorism with a specific means of indicating purpose, and the ability to more accurately predict weapons, methods and targets, as well as overcoming the inherent difficulties in attempting a universal definition of terrorism. The universal definition of terrorism, as it stands, holds little practical use, outside of serving as a broad summary of the phenomenon. Surely, the concern of academics and policy-makers should lie in creating a set of definitions that reflect the variation between motivations and allow for the most effective means of fighting the terrorist threat.

Now, it can be concluded with a quote from the Secretary-General of the United Nations, who was expressing his impatience with the inability of the international community to reach a commonly agreed upon definition. He stated, "I understand that there are outstanding issues, which until now have prevented agreement on this convention. Some of the most difficult issues relate to the definition of terrorism. I understand and accept the need for legal precision. But let me say frankly that there is also a need for moral clarity."[1] He identified the bottom line in the debate on a definition of terrorism, namely, that "there can be no acceptance of those who would seek to justify the deliberate taking of innocent civilian life, regardless of cause or grievance. If there is one universal principle that all peoples can agree on, surely it is this."[2]

References

1. Secretary-General, Addressing Assembly on Terrorism, Calls for Immediate, Far-Reaching Changes' in UN Response to Terror, U.N. Doc. SG/SM/7977, GA/9920, on 1st October, 2001. Retrieved January 30, 2012 from http://www.un.org/News/Press/docs/2001/sgsm7977.doc.htm.

2. *Ibid.*

Index